PENGUIN BOOKS

THE ARCHITECT AND SOCIETY

Edited by John Fleming and Hugh Honour

Palladio

James S. Ackerman, Arthur Kingsley Porter Professor of Fine Arts Emeritus at Harvard University and a Fellow and former Trustee of the American Academy in Rome, was born in San Francisco in 1919 and studied at Yale and New York University. He is a former editor of the *Art Bulletin*, a member of the American Academy of Arts and Sciences, and a corresponding member of the British Academy, the Accademia Olimpica (Vicenza), the Ateneo Veneto and the Royal Academy of Uppsala. He gave the Slade Lectures at Cambridge in 1969–70. In 1985 he was awarded the Order of Merit of the Republic of Italy for his contribution to the history of Italian architecture.

Professor Ackerman has lived several years in Italy, beginning with service during the last war. He is the author of many studies on Italian architecture, including *The Cortile del Belvedere* (1954), a history of the Renaissance portion of the Vatican Palace, and *The Architecture of Michelangelo* (1961), which received the Charles Rufus Morey Award of the College Art Association of America and the Alice David Hitchcock Award of the Society of Architectural Historians, and is also published by Penguin. He is co-author of a volume on historical practice and theory, *Art and Archaeology* (1963). His other books include *The Villa: Form and Ideology of Country Houses* (1990) and a volume of collected essays, *Distance Points* (1991). He has conceived and narrated the films *Looking for Renaissance Rome* (1975, with Kathleen Weil-Garris Brandt) and *Palladio the Architect and His Influence in America* (1980).

Photographs by Phyllis Dearborn Massar.

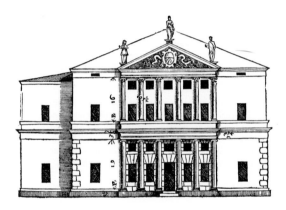

Palladio

by James S. Ackerman

PENGUIN BOOKS

PENGUIN BOOKS

Published by the Penguin Group
Penguin Books Ltd, 80 Strand, London WC2R 0RL, England
Penguin Putnam Inc., 375 Hudson Street, New York, New York 10014, USA
Penguin Books Australia Ltd, Ringwood, Victoria, Australia
Penguin Books Canada Ltd, 10 Alcorn Avenue, Toronto, Ontario, Canada M4V 3B2
Penguin Books (NZ) Ltd, Private Bag 102902, NSMC, Auckland, New Zealand

Penguin Books (NZ) Ltd, Cnr Rosedale and Airborne Roads, Auckland, New Zealand

First published in Pelican Books 1966
Reprinted in Penguin Books 1991

7

Copyright © James S. Ackerman, 1966
All rights reserved

Designed by Gerald Cinamon

Printed and bound in Singapore by Kyodo Printing Co. (S'pore) Pte Ltd
Set in Monotype Garamond

Contents

Contents

Illustrations

Preface

Since Palladio research has been intense lately, and new discoveries are still changing our idea of his work, this is not the time to write a 'definitive' monograph about him. The sort of essay suggested by my editors (I really should say my collaborators) John Fleming and Hugh Honour attempts to portray the architect in several different aspects : his uniqueness as a designer, and in turn his borrowing from the past and present; his education and point of view; and the nature of the cultural and physical environment in which he worked. The approach is indicated by the recent evolution of art history and criticism and reflects the expanded perspectives of the contemporary architect, who has had to look beyond buildings to the larger environments of history, society, landscape and the city. The structure and message would be the same if the book were several times longer and discussed every building and project thoroughly, and I hope that its brevity may recommend it to many readers who lack time or courage to face volumes of more imposing bulk.

For an unencumbered year of looking and writing in Italy I thank the American Council of Learned Societies for a grant, Harvard University for a leave of absence, and the American Academy in Rome for shelter and good fellowship. The Centro Internazionale di Storia dell'Architettura in the Palazzo Valmarana in Vicenza, with its library and *fototeca* and its excellent annual seminar, was the ideal headquarters for study; its Executive Secretary, Renato Cevese, has been a cornucopia of information and ideas, and Vittor Luigi Braga, who undertook the restoration of the palace, a splendid guide. I am grateful to Professors Franco Barbieri, Camillo Semenzato and Wladimir Timofiewitsch, the authors of monographs awaiting publication at the Centre, for their generosity in allowing me to enrich my account with perceptions for which they deserve credit, and to Antonio Dalla Pozza of the Bertoliana Library in Vicenza for sharing his most recent discoveries. I should not have started this study without the stimulus of conversations with Michelangelo Muraro, whose insights and knowledge, especially of the economic and social background, reappear in every chapter. My wife cheerfully read the most boring of the Palladio literature and did her best to keep me from emulating it.

If this book has more than passing value, it will be due to the photographs by Phyllis Massar whose generosity, I hope, will be rewarded by the realization that they reveal Palladio far better than my words.

Rome, 1965

Preface to the Second Edition

The revisions to the original text that I have made on the tenth anniversary of its publication are aimed only to correct those errors called to my attention by reviewers and to alter the dates of buildings and the bibliographical notes to take account of scholarly contributions of the past decade.

The book was conceived prior to the extraordinary burst of scholarship on Palladio and the architecture of the Venetian mainland which was stimulated by the activities and the publications of the Centro Internazionale di studi dell'architettura 'Andrea Palladio' in Vicenza, dating from the early sixties on. Our greatly expanded knowledge of the subject today is finding expression in new and different characterizations of Palladio than the one found here; but I believe that this book remains valid, and I hope that readers will continue to find it illuminating.

Cambridge, Mass., 1976

Acknowledgements

All photographs are by Phyllis Dearborn Massar except the following:

Alinari, 15; author, 1, 4, 14, 45, 86; Bildarchiv Foto Marburg, 74; Brogi, 51; Ferrini, Vicenza, 2, 46, 47, 52; Fiorentini, Venice, 5, 17; Fototecnica, Vicenza, 63, 64; Gabinetto Fotografico Nazionale, 62; Giacomelli, Venice, 8, 9, 77; R. T. McKenna, New York, 79; Sandrini, Vicenza, 49; Soprintendenza ai monumenti, Venice, 96; Vajenti, Vicenza, 48, 50; John Vincent, Berkeley, Calif., 6, 75.

Photographs of the drawings from the Burlington-Devonshire Collection of the Royal Institute of British Architects are from the Corpus Gernsheim and published with Dr Gernsheim's permission.

The Surviving Works of Andrea Palladio

Villas

1540–50

Lonedo, *Godi*, 1537–42
Lonedo, *Piovene* (centre block without
    porch), *c.*1539–40
Montecchio, *Forni-Cerato*, *c.*1540–45
Bertesina, *Gazoto (Gazzotti)-Marcello*,
    early 1540s
Bagnolo, *Pisani*, after 1542
Quinto, *Thiene*, mid-1540s
Finale, *Saraceno*, mid-1540s
Poiana Maggiore, *Poiana*, late 1540s
Caldogno, *Caldogno*, 1548–9

1550–60

Piombino Dese, *Cornaro,* 1551–4
Montagnana, *Pisani*, *c.*1552–5
Vancimuglio, *Chiericati*, mid-1550s
Fratta Polesine, *Badoer*, after 1556
Maser, *Barbaro*, 1557–8
Malcontenta, *Foscari*, 1559–60

1560–70

Lisiera, *Valmarana*, 1563–4
Fanzolo, *Emo*, *c.*1564
Cessalto, *Zeno*, before 1566
Vicenza, *Rotonda*, 1566–70
S. Sofia, *Sarego*, *c.*1568–9

1570–80

Palaces and Public Buildings

1540–50

Vicenza, *Casa Civena,* after 1540
Vicenza, *Palazzo Thiene*, after 1542

Vicenza, *Basilica*, 1549
Vicenza, *Palazzo Iseppo Porto*,
    late 1540s

1550–60

Vicenza, *Palazzo Chiericati*, 1550
Udine, *Palazzo Antonini*, 1556
Udine, *Arco Bollani*, 1556
Feltre, *Palazzo Comunale*, 1557–8

1560–70

Cividale, *Pretorio*, before 1565
Vicenza, *Palazzo Valmarana*, 1565–6
Vicenza, *Palazzo Schio-Angaran*,
    façade, before 1566

1570–80

Vicenza, *Palazzo Barbarano*, 1570–71
Vicenza, *Loggia del Capitaniato*, 1571
Vicenza, *Palazzo Porto-Breganze*, 1570s
San Daniele del Friuli, *Porta Gemona*,
    1579
Vicenza, *Teatro Olimpico,* 1579–80

Ecclesiastical Architecture

1540–50

1550–60

1560–70

Venice, *Sta Maria della Carità*, cloister, 1560–61
Venice, *San Giorgio Maggiore*, refectory, 1560–62; church, 1565
Venice, *San Francesco della Vigna*, façade, after 1562
Vicenza, *Cathedral*, apse, vault, before 1565

1570–80

Vicenza, *Sta Corona, Valmarana Chapel,* 1576
Venice, *Il Redentore,* 1576–7
Venice, *Le Zitelle* (altered), *c.*1579–80
Maser, *Tempietto,* 1579–80

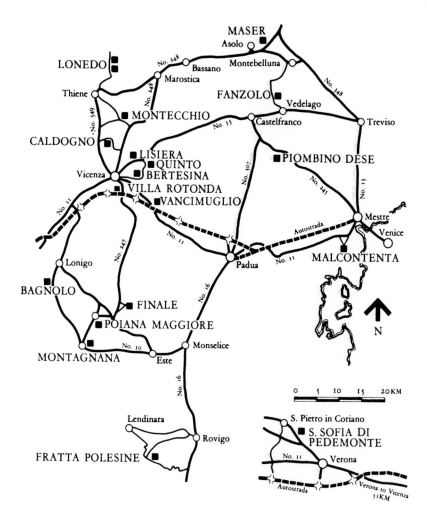

Palladio's villas

Palladio

1: Palladio and His Times

All over the western world, hundreds of thousands of houses, churches and public buildings with symmetrical fronts and applied half-columns topped by a pediment descend from the designs of Andrea Palladio. He is the most imitated architect in history, and his influence on the development of English and American architecture probably has been greater than that of all other Renaissance architects combined.

To many generations his architecture seemed the perfect embodiment of the classical tradition, partly because of its obvious references to Greek and Roman antiquity which in fact are superficial, like the ancient names and words in Renaissance poetry. The essential factor is a sense of order, of the relationship of parts among themselves and to the whole, that Palladio inherited from the great procession of Italian designers from Brunelleschi to Bramante and Michelangelo, and reformulated in a way that distils the Renaissance.

Palladio's birth in Padua in 1508 was perfectly placed and timed. He grew up in the midst of one of the most creative periods in the history of architecture; not at the centre of things, where he might have become just another member of the Roman or Florentine school, but in the one area outside that centre where a Golden Age was in the making, the Republic of Venice. Palladio was a contemporary and collaborator of Veronese, Tintoretto and the sculptor Vittoria, and died only three years after Titian – names that bring to mind rich colour and light and varied textures, peculiarly Venetian luxuries for which Palladio came to invent architectural equivalents.

There was no other first-rate architect of Palladio's generation born and trained in the Veneto; those who came in from outside, like Sansovino and Sanmicheli, adapted the central Italian idiom to the Venetian tradition, but never quite absorbed, as Palladio did, the Byzantine fantasy or the marvellous lightness and radiance of the provincial earlier Renaissance architecture of Venice. The sensuousness of Venetian style was a catalyst that transformed the scholarly and intellectual ingredients of Palladio's thought into the most human architecture of his age, and made it accessible to every succeeding generation.

Andrea di Pietro della Gondola was apprenticed at thirteen to a stone-carver in Padua, but in 1524 he broke his contract, fled to nearby Vicenza [Map] and settled there. For the next fourteen years he worked as an apprentice and assistant to the carvers Giovanni da Pedemuro and Girolamo Pittoni, who did most of Vicenza's monuments and decorative sculpture of this period in an up-to-date style derived from the architecture of Michele Sanmicheli of Verona [5]. At thirty, Andrea must have been the presumptive heir to this modest enterprise, when he had the good luck to be called to the outskirts of town to work on a new loggia and other additions that the Count Giangiorgio Trissino had designed for his Villa at Cricoli [2]. This loggia was the first actual building in Vicenza composed in the classical style of the Roman Renaissance.

Trissino was the pre-eminent intellectual of Vicenza: distinguished for Humanistic studies, a writer of drama, poetry and philological scholarship, he enjoyed sharing his learning, and accepted a number of young nobles into his household as students. As an amateur architect, he followed progress on his villa closely, and this brought him into contact with Andrea, whom he decided to house and to educate together with the younger aristocrats. He also gave him the classical name Palladio, to crown his elevated status; it suggested the wisdom of Pallas Athene, and Trissino had decided to use it for an angelic messenger in his epic poem, *Italia Liberata dai Goti*. That ambitious and uninspired work was dedicated to the Emperor Charles v. Trissino, in spite of his generosity toward Andrea, cultivated a kind of Humanism that was, as Wittkower put it, 'aristocratic and in a way anachronistic; he advocated a formal, esoteric and dogmatic classicism free from any popular tendencies.' Both in the epic and in a fragment that remains of a projected architectural treatise, he shows that he was as interested in architectural theory and ancient remains as in literature and rhetoric. Probably he looked on Palladio as a potential specialist-assistant in this field, and, since he could not hope to give an ignorant stonemason of thirty a rounded classical education, set him to reading only what pertained to architecture, engineering, ancient topography, and military science (in the translation of Caesar's *Commentaries* that Palladio published with the help of his sons, Trissino is cited as his preceptor in tactics). These were to be the fields in which Palladio could quote ancient and modern authorities; he rarely referred to non-architectural writers. He became, in substance, a part-Humanist in the Trissino circle – not an Albertian *uomo universale* such as the Accademia Olimpica, of which he was later to be a founder, sought to encourage, but an early precursor of the modern expert with a penetrating knowledge of the practice and the literature in one discipline, and a casual acquaintance with some others.

When Trissino left Vicenza in 1538 to spend three years in Padua, Palladio may have joined him for part of the time, and in this way may have come to know a still more stimulating dilettante of architecture, Alvise Cornaro, and the Veronese painter Falconetto, whom Cornaro had employed to help him design two garden structures in the court of his palace – a loggia inscribed 1524, and an 'Odeon' for musical performances, of about 1530 [1]. These were the precursors of Villa Cricoli, and the first buildings in the Veneto that tried to emulate the Roman Renaissance. The impression they made on Palladio shows in some of his earliest drawings [44], which have a similar pedantry or self-consciousness, in that the architectural vocabulary learned from ancient and modern Roman architecture is not absorbed effortlessly into its setting. Compared with the easy pictorial interrelation of parts and whole in a mature Palladio façade [62] these seem to be assembled from a repertory of independent units. But it is always awkward to handle new forms for the first time, and Cornaro's garden architecture is full of fresh ideas, most of which must have been his, since Falconetto's independently designed buildings are not nearly as imaginative.

Alvise Cornaro was a great figure in Padua; a successful farmer, a generous patron and a scholar, but one who preferred action to rumination and devoted much of his life to a vigorous campaign for the reclamation of the river deltas along the Adriatic coast, writing books and urgent memoranda on the salvaging of arable areas that ultimately won the support of the Republic.

His brief treatise on architecture is as original as his garden buildings, but it is surprisingly un-Roman and polemically practical; he was impatient with Vitruvius and Humanist theorists because they could not help to build the comfortable, healthy and inexpensive house that everyone needed. His seven rules of building, besides stating some basic structural precepts, confront aesthetic matters such as symmetry and proportion indecisively, but in a spirit that Palladio was to share. They include, as no other Renaissance theory had done, thoughts about furniture and problems of maintenance: the bedroom door, for example, was to be centred so that beds could go on either side opposite windows; moulded terracotta door and window frames are recommended as against the traditional stone for both economy and ease of repair. Even the design of lavatories preoccupied Cornaro. The tone is as antithetical to Trissino's courtly Humanism as it could be, and Palladio must have found it congenial. The traditional element in his own writing is tempered by the same simplicity and common sense. Probably his debt was even greater: Cornaro was the only Renaissance theorist who suggested that frugal patrons might abandon the ancient orders and all traditional ornament in façade design, and Palladio was the only architect of the time who accepted the challenge.

1. Loggia Cornaro [Falconetto]

In the inchoate but unprecedented designs and buildings of this early period he left even window frames without decorative finish [11, 12]. There is other evidence of Cornaro's influence on Palladio: his inclusion, without explanation, of the pediment among the features of the domestic façade, and his distinctions of size, covering, and proportion between the *sala*, or hall, and the *stanze*, or side rooms.

The contribution of the Cornaro-Falconetto circle to Palladio's education in the late 1530s is inseparable from that of Sebastiano Serlio, the Bolognese theorist who had been working in Rome with Baldassare Peruzzi, and had moved to Venice to prepare the first two of his projected seven books on architecture, the fourth and the third, published in 1537 and 1540. Serlio was in Vicenza in 1539 to consult on the Basilica and to design a temporary wooden theatre in the court of one of the Porto palaces. Palladio may or may not have met him, but in any event the books were certainly more inspiring than the man. They were richly illustrated with woodcuts of ancient and modern Roman buildings and inventions, partly inherited from Peruzzi, but mostly his own. These were the first printed books in which the image rather than the word became the chief conveyor of information and style in the arts. Serlio was not one of the Humanists for whom architecture meant scholarship among the ancient sources, but a non-intellectual publicist of ancient and modern design. He must have known or have heard of the work of Andreas Vesalius, who was preparing in Padua at the same moment a similar revolution in scientific literature – an anatomical treatise in which the results of dissections were published in engravings of cadavers and the parts of the body, and explained in a minimum of words. Vesalius also had to reject much of the baggage of Humanistic learning to introduce his innovations. This atmosphere of experiment and of instruction-by-example was more of our time than of the Renaissance.

Serlio's pictures must have lit the imagination of a provincial colleague who had heard of, but had never seen the splendours of Rome. As if to acknowledge his debt, Palladio modelled his own book a few years later on Serlio rather than Alberti and the Vitruvian tradition, and this choice, given the high quality of the work he illustrated, was to make him the most influential architect of the Renaissance. Serlio's own designs, none of which was carried out in Italy, were not strong enough to win the world, but they appealed to Palladio in these few years of growth when he absorbed and used everything new that came to his attention. Specific Serlian motives appear often in the early drawings and buildings. The style in a larger sense was alloyed with those of Cornaro's circle and of Sanmicheli and Sansovino.

Apart from the lessons to be learned from these two Tuscan-trained architects, which were more fundamental and did not show in particular inventions but rather in scale, and a certain sense of space and organization, Palladio's early education was bookish and antiquarian. It came from talking with learned noblemen, from the books of Vitruvius and Serlio, and from a few buildings such as those in Cornaro's garden and the ruins of Verona and Vicenza, that altogether gave an inadequate view of modern and ancient architecture. A first-hand knowledge of Rome was the catalyst required for the making of a mature architecture.

So Palladio became a traveller; from the time he joined Trissino on his first trip to Rome in 1541 (there were others in 1547 and 1554), until the 1570s when age and the burden of work restricted his movement, he frequently was on the road through Italy from Naples to Piedmont and into Provence. Travel was hard and dangerous then, and Palladio claimed to have been worn down by it, but he was driven by the ambition to know ancient architecture well. To us, his interests appear to have been partly scholarly and partly professional, since he used his knowledge for archaeological publications as well as for building, but he would have claimed rather that there was a single body of learning preserved from the past that might be revived either in words or in structures; he even introduced his architectural treatise, the *Quattro Libri*, with the remark that the study of ancient remains is a path to the power and moral force of the ancient Romans.

As he travelled, he sketched and measured the buildings that could be seen above ground, usually in geometric projection (flat), so as to get the most accurate record of the design rather than an impression of the building as it appeared to the eye. He supplemented first-hand knowledge by copying from the sketchbooks of other architects, which probably were the source of most of his perspective sketches. There was a widespread exchange of such records and of ideas among architects, particularly in Rome, interested in uncovering the ancient past. Collaborative effort became easier in about the second decade of the century, when architects began to record measurements on drawings of antiquities.

This information could be turned into illustrations of some kinds of Roman buildings and the details of their ornament, and Renaissance books like Palladio's *Quattro Libri* or his unpublished sketchbooks are full of temples, theatres, bridges, arches and baths. But houses, palaces, villas and basilicas, the full knowledge of which had to await the age of excavation, were hard to visualize and had to be pieced together from literary sources. Written descriptions also were the chief source of information on the planning of the ancient city and the relation of buildings to each other, which is one reason why Palladio's drawings, like those of his predecessors, do not record topographical data beyond the limits of single monuments. They represent the fifteenth-century division between the artists, Alberti excepted, who looked only at the buildings (or more often bits of them) for useable ideas, and the literary men, like the topographer Flavio Biondo who read about the past without studying the remains, but in this way got ideas about how the pieces fit together.

Palladio also knew this literary tradition, but did not fully integrate it with his visual experience. After his last trip to Rome in 1554, he published *Le antichità di Roma*, the first reliable and compact pocket guidebook to ancient remains based on a thorough knowledge of topographical scholarship. In thirty-nine pages, it enumerates and locates monuments both destroyed and preserved, but without explicitly referring to any visual evidence. It was Palladio's contemporary Pirro Ligorio who first joined these strains in a voluminous production of printed maps of ancient Rome and still unpublished manuscripts that became a foundation for modern archaeology. He supplemented the evidence available to his predecessors by inscriptions, sarcophagi, coins, gems and whatever other remains came to hand.

Palladio contributed drawings to the Vitruvius edition and commentary of 1556 by Daniele Barbaro – his companion on the last trip to Rome and his patron at Maser – and, it seems, extensive advice, which is acknowledged in the discussion of the Vitruvian theatre, but surely affected the commentary on structure and details of design in the few religious, civic and private structures that Vitruvius describes. The restored plans and elevations are in the style of Palladio's early maturity. Barbaro's was the first Vitruvius edition illustrated by experts with a command of Roman remains, yet it gives a less accurate introduction to the classical heritage than the *Quattro Libri*, because the buildings Vitruvius knew in the first century B.C. were not the most interesting or the best preserved examples of Roman architecture.

I Quattro Libri dell' Architettura was published in 1570 in Venice. Though its author had a Humanist education of a kind, and shared the ideals of his teachers and patrons, it is not a Humanist book. Scholarship and ancient tradition are outweighed by practical know-how expressed in economical and forceful language. The four parts: fundamentals of architecture and the orders; domestic design, mostly Palladio's own; public and urban design and engineering; and temples, were addressed to the

2. Cricoli, Villa Trissino

practising architect whether amateur or professional who was more interested in building than in theory. As the purpose was rather to simplify than to extend the understanding of ancient architecture, Palladio glossed over conflicts between Vitruvian laws of design and the actual buildings, and differences in practice among the buildings themselves. He relied on his woodblocks – an imprecise means of reproduction – to teach useable measurements and proportions.

Palladio's designs of the 1540s and early 1550s show that he found as much in the modern as in the ancient buildings on his first trips to Rome; not the most modern, of Antonio da Sangallo, Peruzzi and others, but those of the Roman Renaissance of the first two decades of the century. Bramante and Raphael, who came from Urbino, were outside the refined and well-established tradition of Tuscan Quattrocento architecture, which perhaps made them more able to absorb the grandiose element in ancient architecture. They were the first methodical surveyors of the ruins. Their work had a classical authority, a way of expressing mass, of modulating light and of transforming voids into positive volumes of space different enough from earlier architecture to prompt contemporary critics to attribute to them the true renaissance of antiquity.

Like Serlio, Palladio included Bramante's Tempietto of 1502 among his ancient temples, not as a good copy of the past, which it wasn't, but as a work of equivalent spirit and stature. So the *kind* of relationship these buildings established to the past affected Palladio as much as their specific innovations, though these, which had already been brought north by Sanmichele and others, impressed him, too. The palace/house façade formula of two storeys without a court and tall balconied windows in the *piano nobile*, definitively stated in Bramante's design of 1513 for the house in which Raphael lived, was fundamental in Palladio's evolution. He drew it [3] in an angle view which shows that he was struck most by the robust

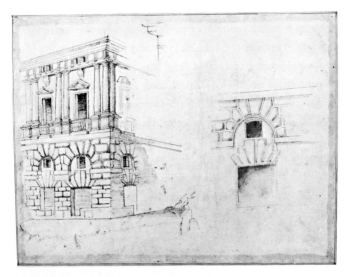

3. House of Raphael [Bramante]

three-dimensionality both of the block itself and of the motives that artic-
ulated it; he was not interested in the composition or proportion of the
whole, in which there was no notable central emphasis. The first-hand experience of this palace and a number of others like it by Raphael and later
followers is evident in Palladio's shift from the flatness of the Casa
Civena and looseness of the early drawing [45, 44] to the design of his
mature palaces [58, 62, 63]. But it was only in this narrow range that
Palladio depended on Bramante's circle; except in Palazzo Thiene [47],
he was not attracted by Roman innovations in planning and, though he
measured and drew the plan of Raphael's Villa Madama, he did not borrow
from it. His palace plans came from reading Vitruvius and, by the time he
designed his first church in 1565, the Roman experience was too far behind to be useful. The villas are untouched by the tradition of central
Italy.

Raphael's assistant, Giulio Romano, who left Rome for Mantua in 1523, powerfully affected Palladio's design in the 1540s with his dramatic and often expressionistic transformations of the Rustic order. Motives identical to Giulio's buildings appear in the elevations of Palazzo Thiene [51, 48] and a number of drawings, but they disappear from Palladio's work after 1550.

Palladio had little chance to know Michelangelo's extraordinary innovations; when he left Rome for the last time in 1554, he could have seen only the stairways of the Capitoline Hill and Vatican Belvedere, the cornice and court windows of the Palazzo Farnese, and perhaps the model of St Peter's without a dome. If St Peter's or the Capitoline Hill suggested the giant order of Palladio's Palazzo Valmarana [58, 61], they did not affect the overall design. Palladio probably was repelled by the bizarre element in the work of Michelangelo.

These great figures of the first decades of the century drew Palladio first in one direction, and then in another, in the formative years, 1538–49, and his work was more erratic in style and quality than that of any apprentice to the profession in the Renaissance. But he matured with unpredictable suddenness; the designs of around 1549 – Palazzo Chiericati [52] and the villas Thiene [37, 36] and Rotonda [31] – were wholly his and wholly new. He had learned to find himself by knowing others.

In the later sixteenth century Italy and all of Europe caught the academic fever. An academy, which in Trissino's time had been a regular gathering of literate friends in a villa garden, rapidly evolved into an elaborate and official institution for sharing and propagating learning. The Accademia Olimpica, one of the earliest, was chartered in Vicenza in 1555 by a group of twenty-one local scholars, mathematicians, a few forward-looking aristocrats, and one artist, Palladio, for the cultivation of the arts and sciences, but especially of mathematics, 'the true ornament of all who possess noble and virtuous spirits'. A year later, the more prosperous nobles, including most of Palladio's patrons, formed another, exclusively aristocratic, Accademia dei Costanti, to foster learning but also to sustain the chivalric tradition in part by staging tournaments and other courtly festivities.

The separation was one symptom of the evolution of a new social conformation in which technicians, scholars and artists emerged from classrooms and shops to become gentlemen, or at least courtiers, while gentlemen put off their armour and merchants abandoned the sea to cultivate the arts with the help of the parvenu experts. In Italy, the change was not really a step toward democracy, but an association of convenience fostered by the dominance of foreign powers that squashed the initiative and individualism of the Renaissance entrepreneur and created a leisure class in need of respectable amusement. As a rule, artists were not welcome in the patrician academies, and formed their own, as in Venice and Florence, to qualify them for intercourse with their patrons and to complete their liberation from shops and guilds. But Vicenza was an exception because it was small and provincial, and because it had no court. Ultimately, the separation of classes could not be maintained there : the Costanti, unequal to their name, disbanded after nine years, and some of them joined the Olimpica, which still survives today.

Palladio would not have qualified for membership had it not been for his association with Trissino and Barbaro, which made him an academician *avant la lettre*. Yet he must have discovered new realms of learning in an institution that paid one of its founding members, Palladio's friend Sylvio Belli, for three lectures a week on Mathematics, which invited speakers on the origin of the winds, on a geographic sphere, and on Good Government, and which sponsored poetry readings, concerts, and above all, theatrical performances. The success of the last led in 1579–80 to the construction of an academic building on Palladio's design, the principal feature of which was a theatre (pp. 179–182, [95, 96]). The Teatro Olimpico is

4. Library of San Marco [J. Sansovino]

a sort of academic discourse in three dimensions, a learned reconstruction of the ancient Roman theatre based on a lifetime of study of monuments and texts. Certainly archaeological curiosity overshadowed architectural invention in the design of the theatre, and what makes it fascinating today is its capacity rather to recreate a Humanist-antiquarian ambience than to move the visitor by its forms and spaces.

Palladio's first encounters with Venice were discouraging. He lost a competition for a government post in 1554, and, in the following year, Sansovino's design for the Scala d'Oro in the Doge's Palace was preferred to his. None of his designs for Venetian Palaces (e.g., *Quattro Libri*, II, 71, 72, and [62]) was put to use, and the grandiose scheme for a bridge at the Rialto, probably of the late 1560s, also was rejected in favour of a Sansovino project that was cancelled by the Turkish war. Before 1570, Palladio's Venetian work was all ecclesiastical. But the death of Sansovino in that year abruptly changed the climate and Palladio became his successor *de facto*. He held no official position but, being abler than those who did, he gained the best commissions both public and private, and had to move his family to Venice in 1570 or 1571.

In the following year he lost his two eldest sons, and afterwards he seems to have lived a secluded life. Apart from publishing Caesar's *Commentaries* with their illustrations as a memorial, he apparently abandoned his studies and his ambitions as an author, though he kept up his Humanist associations, particularly with the nobleman Giacomo Contarini, the heir to his drawings. In these years there is no visible link between Palladio's experiences or environment and his work, as there had been earlier. He did not become more Venetian for living there, though Venice became more Palladian.

Of the numerous church and monastery commissions of the seventies, none was carried out according to plan except the grandest of all, Il Redentore, sponsored by the government itself. The civil work – advice on fortifications, a triumphal arch and decorations at the Lido for the reception of Henry III of France, and the redecoration of rooms in the Doge's palace after the fires of 1574 and 1577 – was bureaucratic and produced no important building. For the latter, Palladio designed ceilings and portals in the state rooms familiar to all tourists, but most of his work was drowned out by the lavish Venetian arpeggios of sculptors and stuccoists. In Venice only the Redentore survives unaltered as the fruit of this productive and lucrative decade of work.

Palladio was sincerely religious, and a devoted husband and father who gave his sons a gentleman's education – one became a lawyer – and his daughter a handsome dowry, though he remained poor until his later years. Vasari describes him as particularly well liked by his contemporaries. Paolo Gualdo, who wrote a brief biography in 1616, writes that he 'was especially pleasant and entertaining in conversation and greatly delighted the gentlemen and lords with whom he dealt as well as the labourers he employed, who always were kept happy and working contentedly by his many pleasantries.' None of the several portraits said to represent Palladio has an unassailable pedigree.

5. Palazzo Pompei [Sanmicheli]

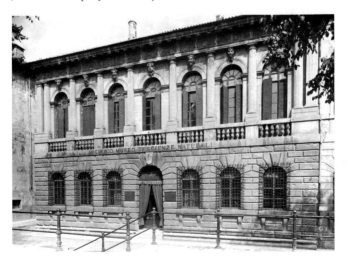

2: Villas

Palladio's early palace designs depended on the innovations of Bramante and other Romans, but his villas were rooted in a culture distinct from that of central Italy. They form a style apart, vital and never diminishing in the capacity to entice others into emulation, but evasive of definition. Among the twenty surviving villas and twenty-odd projects known from drawings and the *Quattro Libri*, there are few instances of a repeated plan, motive or composition in mass; Palladio would produce at most two or three versions of a particular scheme before reaching out in an entirely new direction. The common core within this variety is a particular conception of architectural harmony and composition. There is, then, no 'typical' Palladian villa; but by studying a large one that was finished according to plan, like the Barbaro villa at Maser [6, 8], one begins to see what makes a Palladio villa unique, and different from a characteristic contemporary Roman one like Pirro Ligorio's villa in Tivoli, built for Cardinal Ippolito d'Este in the 1560s [7].

The Tivoli villa was a convenient place to which an overworked executive might retire for rest. The air is fresh, one is not hemmed in by buildings and noise, and green things grow about. But it is not real country, even though it is built away in the hills, because – except for distant views of the Roman Campagna – nature is excluded by high walls, and the ingeniously devised garden makes greenery behave in as elegant and unnatural a fashion as a courtier at the Vatican.

Maser, on the other hand, is far away from society; it is not a suburban retreat but the principal dwelling of its builders. It is elevated sufficiently from the surroundings to give a view of the fields and orchards of the estate, but effectively it is *in* the fields. If the contemplation of nature or of ingenious gardening had been an important aspect of its function, it easily could have been perched high on its hill-side. Further, it is invitingly

6. Villa Barbaro

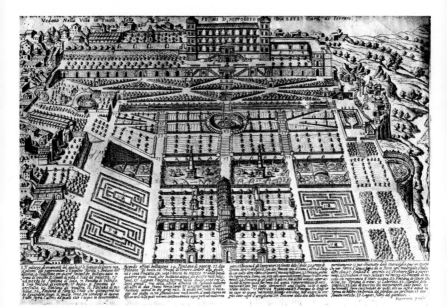

open to the out-of-doors; part of the dwelling unit juts forward to catch the light from three sides, and is flanked by long arcades in which the farm equipment and animals were kept. There were dovecots up under the arches. This is the great difference from the Tivoli villa: Maser really functions as a farm. Daniele and Marcantonio Barbaro were not there simply to get away from the heat and the gondolas of Venice, but to make sure that the crops were good; the luxury in which they lived was dependent on those crops. But they were as far from being rustics as was the Cardinal. They were born in Venice of aristocrats whose money came from overseas commerce, and were educated in Humanist schools and the University at Padua. Daniele, apart from being the editor of Vitruvius, Aristotelian scholar, writer on perspective, mathematician, and ambassador, had been nominated Patriarch of Aquilea by the Republic. Both brothers were more men of the world than the other gentlemen farmers, and Maser reflects their interests by being the most richly and handsomely decorated sixteenth-century villa in north Italy.

Behind the main block and the smelly arcades on a terrace at the height of the *piano nobile*, there is an enclosed court with an antiquarian's nymphaeum [8] like those Ligorio and his contemporaries were building in Rome, its niches filled with stuccoed statues by Alessandro Vittoria representing the deities of Olympus, each identified by an epigram. Vittoria also sculpted the façade reliefs and niche statues; these, and the free-standing figures about the garden, represent ancient gods and allegories.

Inside, every room of the upper level was frescoed by Paolo Veronese at the height of his career [9]. The scenes are from ancient mythology, poetic allegory and contemporary country life of the aristocracy. Many landscapes imitating ancient perspective murals were painted as if one looked through the walls over painted balconies to distant prospects, some with romantic ruins; and there are frescoed doors that seem to open to reveal members of the family and staff entering the real space of the rooms.

Veronese's world is almost independent of the actual architecture. It removes the walls and carries on in a brilliant space beyond. Is this why Palladio, always scrupulous in crediting his collaborators, failed to mention Veronese ? If so, it is a sad irony, because they were perfect collaborators, both able to immerse themselves in antiquity but to make of it something wholly original; both masters of a new light and colour. To the extent that architecture and painting can be compared, their styles were alike, and much more alike than either was to Vittoria's.

In short, like most of Palladio's villas, Maser represented the best of two worlds, the farmer's and the gentleman's. This union was quite new in Renaissance architecture, and its sudden appearance demands an explanation. Knowing of Palladio's Vitruvian studies under Trissino's guidance, we should expect his villas of those early years to be typical antiquarian essays, and it is surprising to find that they can be less so than most of his later work. There are usually more references to the ancient orders in medieval buildings than in the Villa Godi, for example, designed before 1540 [10], or in the contemporary drawings [12] of which there are several quite stripped of ornament. Nothing of the kind happened in Palladio's palace design: his earliest façade sketches and the Casa Civena [45], done shortly after the Villa Godi, show an effort to control the style of the Roman Renaissance as it had filtered through the north Italian architects of the previous generation. At least half of the villa designs follow this typically Renaissance direction, which seems the natural one for an artist who had spent the previous sixteen years carving details of just the sort that he now was eliminating from the Villa Godi group. A villa of the same period, at Bertesina, near Vicenza [13], is the more expected outcome of the contact with Trissino, Padua [1, 2] and Serlio. Always a lover of symmetry, Palladio carefully balanced two antithetical

8. Villa Barbaro, nymphaeum

9. Villa Barbaro, interior

styles, of which the stripped, cubistic one was the more original and exciting.

This style, which was encouraged by Cornaro's ideas of economic domestic design, was contrary to the Humanist tradition, but still was inspired by ancient Rome – not the Rome of Vitruvius, but the Rome without Hellenistic roots, of simple structures made by the engineers and untouched by the decorators, such as the exterior of the Pantheon (which has a cornice supported by the same kind of modillions as the villas in Lonedo) or the baths [92], which are the source of the 'thermal' windows of [12] and pediments with broken bases in some of the sketches now in London. The plans of [12] and similar villas also recall the baths. These projects, generally assigned to the period before Palladio's first visit to Rome because of the absence of ancient ornament, should rather be placed at least in part afterwards. Ancient ornament could have been studied in provincial examples or in the sketchbooks of other architects, but the stripped style of antiquity had never been noticed before, and Palladio could have found and recorded it only by discovering it for himself.

While the drawings show a conscious engagement with the pragmatic structures of antiquity, the early villas themselves are bound unconsciously to an ancient tradition that did not need to be revived in the Renaissance because it had survived without a break from the Roman Empire. The similarity in plan between the Villa Godi and Villa Trissino [10, 2] – a three-bay loggia flanked by two projecting tower-like blocks – may be due in part to Palladio's studies with Trissino, but the same massing could have been discovered in any of a number of older country houses in the Veneto or, for that matter, in Rome or Tuscany. In fact, it was the characteristic form of the few Venetian villas that survive from the later fifteenth and early sixteenth century [15], and the only thing that Trissino added was a Roman Renaissance vocabulary, which is precisely what Palladio did not do in his first villa.

10. Villa Godi

The smaller provincial villas of the landed gentry of late Roman antiquity were nearly all of this kind, and they have been found in modern excavations throughout the Empire. In the years of the barbarian invasions, when it was no longer safe to live in the countryside, these structures disappeared. But they had already found their way into the repertory of Byzantine architecture, and reappeared in the form of Venetian palaces and commercial structures such as the Turkish Warehouse or Fondaco of the thirteenth century [14]. They appeared in Venice not only because of its close commercial ties with Constantinople, but because it was a city defended and fortified by water, so that throughout the later Middle Ages its buildings could be designed for display and openness rather than for defence. The characteristic Venetian palace was created on this model; later, when the mainland again became habitable, the Venetians returned, bringing back to the land the building type that they unknowingly had borrowed from it. Possibly some of the Renaissance villas, Palladio's included, rest on the ruins of their late Imperial forerunners.

The Villa Trissino in Cornedo, south of Vicenza, is a modest example of this type from the fifteenth century, and a more imposing and self-conscious one is the great Colleoni villa in Thiene [15], which is much like its urban relatives on the Grand Canal, with its great Gothic five-arched window set in a rectangular frame like a painted altarpiece. While many of the smaller villas were little more than fancy farmhouses and open to the fields, the Colleoni was a *casa signorile* which still had to be protected with a high medieval *castello* wall. It was reasonably safe to build on the Terrafirma in 1490, but it was not safe enough to expose yourself to the landscape on all sides as the Barbaros or Emos could do half a century later. A number of villa views of around 1500, starting with those sketched by Marin Sanudo into his *Itinerary through the Venetian Terrafirma* of 1483, illustrate the characteristic *castello* layout. The site often is elevated, since the wealthy

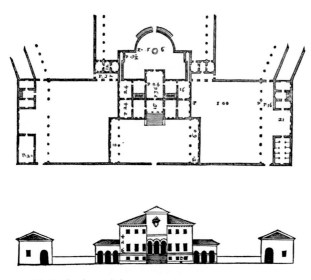

11. Villa Godi, plan and elevation

owner was likely to build more to enjoy the landscape than to profit from cultivating it; a towered and crenellated castle is pictured at the centre surrounded at a distance by high walls with a single towered gateway [16]. Within the walls there is a formal pergola'd garden, a court for farming equipment and produce, and ordinary structures for housing peasants, animals, and wine. In a castle garden like this, the courtly lovers of Bembo's *Gli Asolani* walked and whispered.

Between this moment and the early studies of Palladio came a period of experimentation based on castle, urban and rustic forerunners. Most of the surviving villas were small in scale and the majority must have been built without the aid of architects; they have the vital inventiveness of an unselfconscious culture. Palladio assimilated and brought order to this directionless trend. His first villa, at Lonedo [11], is perched like a *castello* on the mountain-side, and not in easily managed farmland; it is a walled compound that has a forecourt before the owner's house which is isolated from two service courts alongside; in the rear there is a walled garden. But the walls were not meant to be high enough to block the view; they gave only a symbolic protection. This castello-like enclosure appears in all of Palladio's early projects that include more than the dwelling itself, though the dwelling was sometimes put on the periphery of the enclosure, with one side exposed. Later, protective walls disappeared entirely, and the villa opened defencelessly to the world about. The walled compound resembles the central Italian suburban practice of the previous century, and it recalls what Alberti had to say in describing his ideal villa, which was based on a fusion of ancient sources and medieval practice.

At the same time, the two greatest architects in north Italy attempted to create a modern villa form based on the Tuscan tradition but suited to the Veneto: Michele Sanmicheli, who was trained by Antonio da Sangallo the Younger, and Jacopo Sansovino, a Florentine who had been adopted by the Venetians. Sanmicheli's La Soranza, of *c.* 1550 – now destroyed – was another loggia-villa with projecting side wings; the older architect may have been swayed by Palladio's early work. Sansovino's villa in Ponte-casale [17], on the other hand, was something apart. Away in the dreary Adige delta, soaked by rain and fog and battered by sun, it represented a beautiful aberration in the evolution of architecture that was to have no progeny. Sansovino envisaged the country villa that he built for the Garzoni family in the later 1540s as a rural palace of noble dimensions. Like the other villas in the Venetian tradition, it has the familiar central loggia and side blocks, but it is somehow too aulic for the country, like a Doge at a swimming hole. Pictures give no conception of its commanding charm, particularly in the interior court, which also has rather an urban air; yet a visit is to be recommended only to the enthusiast; even today the roads are bad and it is a long way from civilization. The villa is the earliest manifestation of an entirely new direction in rural building which cannot be explained by the favourite tool of art-historical deduction, the analysis of style. It was not an eccentricity of aristocratic taste that drove the Garzoni, and later the Emos and Barbaros, into the country, but a force strong enough to outweigh its patent social and physical disadvantages, and a new force, which had not moved their ancestors. That it was economic in nature we can gather from the size, prominence and proximity of the functional farm structures: those long arcaded barns – *barchesse* in Venetian usage – that Palladio later integrated into the building itself.

A generation ago, the economy of sixteenth-century Venice was described as decaying at a steady rate as war, foreign competition and the stagnation of the aristocracy gradually choked off sources of income. It was said that the capital amassed in fifteenth-century trade was wasted in luxury – fancy clothes, pictures by Veronese and Tintoretto, country villas in which to enjoy a lazy degeneracy. That there is a flaw in this picture, particularly with respect to country life, we might guess from the visual evidence alone: one does not build effete pleasure-domes in swamplands, far from society, and surrounded by animals and fowl.

Lately, a lively school of Venetian economic historians has shown that it was a more radical social change that drew the aristocracy to the country. Without minimizing the decay of the Venetian mercantile economy, they reveal that the aristocrats of the Republic did not degenerate in the later sixteenth century, but were able to create economic defences against the pressures of the new giant states of Western Europe and, in 1571, to defeat superior Turkish forces at Lepanto and contain the Muslim advance into the Mediterranean. But the success could be only temporary: Venice was exhausted from the wars of the early sixteenth century. As these subsided, the effects of the Renaissance voyages of discovery began to be felt in Europe; gold flowed from America into Spain and Portugal, creating inflation in the Mediterranean and abetting two major bank failures in Venice. Countries of the Atlantic seaboard began to trade with India by sea, and challenged Venice's caravan markets in the Levant; even in the Mediterranean, the English outflanked Venice with a merchant fleet

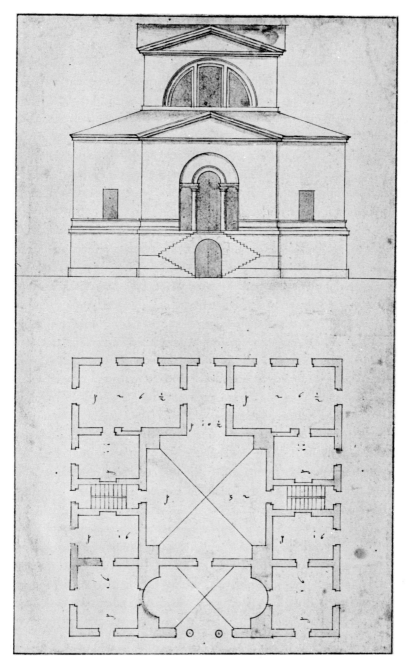

12. Villa project

that evaded pirates and Turks by speed rather than the heavy armament that made the Venetian ships obsolete. If Venice had revised the laws that restricted membership in her oligarchic government to the old families, and if she had opened her market to traders of other countries, she might have postponed her economic decline by perhaps a generation, but it was inevitable that a Renaissance city-state should ultimately be overwhelmed by the great empires of the seventeenth-century monarchs. What is relevant for the moment, however, is that by private and communal effort that event was deferred for half a century.

After 1530 the capitalist nobility of Venice, which had made fabulous fortunes in commerce in the fifteenth century, began to protect itself from the risks of trade and the instability of exchange by seeking more stable investments : on the one hand in a revival of industry, particularly of cloth and luxury goods, and on the other hand in large-scale acquisitions of agricultural properties. Venetians had held land on the terrafirma in the preceding century, but, cultivated by medieval methods, and in large part swampy and malaria-ridden, it had had no economic significance. Now, however, the economic potentialities of agriculture began to appear more attractive, and meanwhile its development became urgent as the population grew beyond the point that could be sustained without importing grain on an inflated market. Three important innovations were necessary to a productive agricultural economy : a shift from a low-grade cereal to the cultivation of corn from Turkey, vast projects of land-reclamation, and the distribution of unused public and private lands among investors willing to cultivate them.

Corn meant a healthier diet for the peasant and, because it took more and different care than lesser cereals, promoted improved methods of farming. Reclamation, involving water control – chiefly by canals and sea-walls – in the swamplands and deltas throughout the terrafirma, brought about a radical change ; state or private investment companies took over

13. Villa Gazoto-Marcello

14. Fondaco dei Turchi

land rescued from the water and accelerated the breakup of feudal holdings. In 1556 the Venetian senate passed a bill creating the Board of Uncultivated Properties and empowered it to subsidize reclamation and to co-ordinate the projects of private individuals and consortiums that had emerged on models proposed by Cornaro. In seventy years between 1510 and 1580 the tax yield from terrafirma property increased four hundred per cent.

This kind of agricultural revolution could not be carried out by peasants: it needed able administrators and astute financiers, since reclamation was risky even with government support, and also the investors had to be on hand to direct the work. As the Pisani, the Badoers and the Emos committed their fortunes to the land, they were no more inclined to delegate the responsibility of administering them than had their fathers been inclined to hire professional sailors to trade for them in the Levant. Within thirty years, between 1530 and 1560, many Venetian and terrafirma landowners moved onto their estates, selecting sites central to their holdings, and often, as at Bagnolo, alongside the newly tamed waterways [19].

Here they needed houses for their families, retainers and animals radically different from those of the medieval country castle. To design them, they needed an architect who had come to maturity in the 1530s, who would survive until the decline of the building bubble in the deflationary period around 1570, who would possess a skill rare in the Renaissance, in designing functional and utilitarian structures for which there was no tradition in earlier architecture, but who would command the classical heritage so as to lend an air of cultivated grandeur to the country estate of gentlemen who still thought like city dwellers, and finally, who would know how to build cheaply as well as grandly. That was Palladio: 'had he not existed he would have to have been invented'. In a sense, he was invented. If the quasi-country gentleman, Trissino, had not drawn him out of the stoneyard at the dawn of the agricultural revolution, he would not have been Palladio, much less an architect. The times made the man. Luckily, the man was a genius.

The economic situation affected the villa initially in determining its site. It dictated isolated areas rather than those where cultivation had gone on for centuries: uninhabited delta and swamplands where the chances for lucrative reclamation were good, and where newcomers could acquire large consolidated holdings. It suggested building sites central to the agricultural functions and a building programme that drew service structures and dwelling into one complex, as they had been in common peasants' farms for millennia, and as they are described by the ancient authors who dealt with farm management such as Cato, Varro, and Virgil.

That these determinants do not of themselves produce a Palladian villa is demonstrated by their effect on Sanmicheli and Sansovino [17], who chose to build country palaces separate from the barn arcades. Raised in the Tuscan tradition, they thought in terms of separate blocks, while a Venetian would think in terms of visual continuities (consider the Cathedral area in Pisa in comparison to Piazza San Marco). A kind of urbanistic thinking prompted Palladio to draw together the discrete functions of the villa into a compact organism; he wrote in the *Quattro Libri* that a house 'is nothing other than a small city'.

Behind this metaphor there was a social theory of architectural history: man, according to Palladio, first lived and built alone, but later, seeing the benefits of commerce, he formed villages by bringing houses together and still later, cities by drawing villages together. By analogy, a farm centre would become more economical and natural as its functions were drawn together. Mere clustering, however, would not do. Palladio believed in a hierarchy of functions, and compared the dwelling to the human body, the noble and beautiful parts of which the Lord ordained to be exposed, and the ignoble but essential parts to be hidden from sight. The metaphor of

15. Villa Colleoni

the organism reminds us that every Palladian work is designed as if members are joined symmetrically to a central spine. Whether or not the villas were planned consciously to be built outward in symmetrical units from the spine – as against being raised all at once, storey by storey – this process proved to be eminently suited to the uncertain economy of the time. The master's dwelling had to be made habitable, but from there on Palladio's patrons added just what they could afford of the annexed loggias and towers.

There are typological patterns among the villas : one has two major storeys and pedimented porches with open colonnades on both levels, as at Villa Cornaro in Piombino Dese [18] or the *villa suburbana* Pisani at Montagnana [20]. These, and the Villa Malcontenta [21–24], which is similar except that its porch is of one storey on a high base, were not given extensions for agricultural services, nor were the attics planned for grain storage, as at Poiana Maggiore [25]. Why does this group differ in this respect ? The sites are surely agricultural ; perhaps the owner's property was dispersed in small parcels, as sometimes happened, or the major area of cultivation was distant from the villa and less suited for habitation, so that barns and service structures would have been built out in the fields. Palladio explained that the outermost blocks of the first two were designed for kitchens and storage functions, which usually were put in the basement, so the type may have been invented for swampy areas where everything had to be above ground level; hence the full two-storey elevation and the more vertical form of the block.

The Cornaro and Pisani villas each have two halls, one over the other in the centre of the building. But in the Malcontenta Palladio took advantage of the form of the block to make a two-storey hall [24] with all the grandeur of a Roman bath, which simple furniture makes all the more majestic ; such spaces are rarely found in domestic architecture.

A second type has a central block with one major storey, a central temple-front contained within the block, and attached colonnaded or arcaded wings for farming functions. The villas Barbaro at Maser [6] and Emo at Fanzolo [26, 27, 91] are similar examples, and the Badoer at Fratta Polesine [28, 29] has curved wings that start at a flight of steps a little before the façade; these curves were to become exceedingly popular among eighteenth-century imitators. The Barbaro and the Emo villas were so much more luxurious, particularly in their internal decorations, than the others, that they might seem to have been built rather for pleasure than for work, if the long arcades with their dovecots were not so distinctly agricultural in intention (and identified as such in Palladio's description). They are luxurious because their owners were rich, and that is also why they were finished according to plan, as most of the other villas were not. Daniele Barbaro was an urban gentleman, but while he may not have known his crops, his interests in machinery and engineering probably made him a good farmer anyhow (for example, the water for the garden fountain at Maser [8] was directed into the kitchen for washing and from there to the garden for irrigation).

Apart from these groups, there were designs unique not only in Palladio's work, but in all Renaissance architecture. One is the Villa Sarego in Santa Sofia near Verona [30], which was less than half-finished; its extraordinary wall-less elevation has the vigour of an Egyptian temple. The load borne by the columns demanded that they be of stone, which is exceedingly rare in Palladio's work; he chose drums of irregular depth and breadth and carved them with an expressive force equalled only by Michelangelo.

The combination of the unique plan and elevation of Villa Sarego and its geographical isolation from other villas of Palladio [Map] raises the question of whether geography influenced distinctions in type. The map gives only negative answers. The early stripped style without the columnar

17. Villa Garzoni [J. Sansovino]

18. Villa Cornaro

porch appears in a cluster around Lonedo (villas Godi, Piovene and Cerato in Montecchio), but also at Poiana; the taller two-storey block without agricultural wings is scattered from Malcontenta to Montagnana and to Piombino, and the single-storey type with extended wings is even more dispersed (Fanzolo, Fratta Polesine, Maser). But a disguised rationale that could be called cultural-geographical seems to sustain the typology: the first group, which is more conservative in style, was designed for Vicentines; the last two for Venetians. Also the Rotonda type, built in Vicenza for a hilltop view [33], was repeated only once, and for Vicentines, Francesco and Lodovico Trissino [35]. By this rationale, Villa Sarego is different not because it is distant, but because it is Veronese. The same local specialization of interest partly explains why Palladio built no palaces in Venice and no churches except for Venetians. Admittedly the pattern cannot be seen as a rule; the taste and practical requirements of the nobility might differ from town to town in the Veneto, but common bonds were strong, and the lesser villas not mentioned here cannot be classified so distinctly.

All these villas except the last have in common a pedimented temple front, designed as a porch that projects from or recedes into the block, or simply is laid upon it as a relief. In the architecture surviving from antiquity, this feature appears only as a façade for religious structures. It was adapted to villa architecture first by the Florentine Giuliano da Sangallo for the Medici villa at Poggio a Caiano outside Florence, but the motif was not repeated by Renaissance designers before Palladio. Palladio was the one who made it a hallmark of his work and a leitmotive of post-Renaissance architecture. Humanist clients, who were alert to the implications of architectural motives borrowed from the ancients, would never have allowed their domestic aspirations to be expressed through religious symbolism. If they had associated the pedimented porch only, or even principally, with temples, they would have seen that it violated

19. Bagnolo, Villa Pisani, river front

20. Montagnana, Villa Pisani, garden façade

21. Villa Foscari, river front

Vitruvian *Decorum*, but Palladio, in an apologia for the use of the pediment, referred again to that theory of history according to which the institutions of society, and hence its structures, were formed out of family units. So the house preceded the temple and gave it its form:

In all the villas and also in some of the city houses I have put a frontispiece on the forward façade where the principal doors are because such frontispieces show the entrance of the house, and add very much to the grandeur and magnificence of the work, the front being thus made more eminent than the other parts. Besides, they prove to be especially useful for the builders' coats of arms, which usually are put in the middle of façades. The ancients also used them in their buildings, as may be seen in the remains of temples and of other public edifices. And, as I said in the preface to the first book, it is very likely that they got the invention and the concept from private buildings, that is, from houses. Vitruvius in the last chapter of his third book instructs us how to make them. (*Quattro Libri*, II, p. 69, Ch. xvi.)

Palladio's terms, 'grandeur and magnificence', reveal his wish to ennoble and classicize the villa sufficiently to compensate the learned gentleman who commissioned it for his rustic exile. Often the porch is the only antique reference in the design; all the rest of the detail is simple geometry, which is consistent with the concept of a hierarchy of elements.

22. Villa Foscari, plan

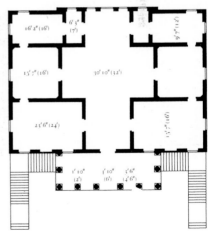

The simplicity also is economically determined; it was cheaper to limit classical ornament to a minimum. Palladio's villas were built of rough brickwork with a coating of stucco; for the most part even the columns were of brick. Stonecarving was reserved for the most refined details such as the bases and capitals of columns and window frames; that it was slow work requiring highly skilled labour was reason enough to limit classical references to one portion of the building. If Palladio's clients had had more exuberant tastes and greater wealth, there probably would not have been enough stone sculptors to handle the building boom on the terrafirma in the period 1550-70. Besides, stucco surfaces and detailing must have appealed to the colour-loving Venetians; they had to be tinted and the colours could be changed at the owner's pleasure. One reason that Palladio's villas have not appeared more often in picture books is that weather-beaten stucco looks shoddy. Some of the villas that now seem to be irredeemable wrecks could be patched, painted and made habitable at a plausible cost.

In the most famous of Palladio's villas, the so-called Rotonda in the suburbs of Vicenza, the classical porch is not used in the usual way; it appears on all four sides, and so it cannot act as the climax of a hierarchy [31, 32]. Hierarchy is still there, though it has its climax at the core, in the form of a dome [33]. Domes also are associated with religious architecture, though their domestic origin, documented by modern archaeology and even by the etymology of the English word (from *domus*), may have been guessed by Palladio. Anyway, he knew that they were not exclusively churchly, because he made the one at the Baths of Caracalla the focus of his restoration drawings. At the Rotonda, the dome was used because it carried the air of monumentality; like the temple front, it is divorced from functional allusions to become a symbol of grandeur.

Three features of the Rotonda set it apart from other Palladian villas:

25. Villa Poiana, entrance

it is very near a town, the site is on a hilltop, and it has no utility buildings. Palladio said of it:

> I have not discussed it among the villas because it is so close to the city. The site is one of the most agreeable and delightful that may be found, because it is on a hillock with gentle approaches, and is surrounded by other charming hills that give the effect of a huge theatre, and they are all cultivated . . . . And because it enjoys the most lovely views on all sides, some screened, others more distant, and others reaching the horizon, loggias were made on each face.

It is not, then, a villa at all, in the sense that the others are, but a *belvedere*. And, in fact, it was built not by a gentleman farmer, but by a retired Monsignore, who used it for parties. Palladio designed it as if its chief function were to promote gazing at the scenery; as this is done by standing on a hilltop and turning in four different directions – each one taking in about ninety degrees at a time – he started with a circle and

26. Villa Emo, central pavilion

27. Villa Emo, arcade

28. Villa Badoer

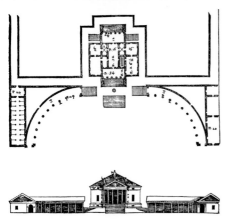

29. Villa Badoer, plan and elevation

extended it radially to four lookouts. The one thing it has in common with other Palladian villas is that the viewer was not regaled by the moods of rugged nature but by the orderly patterns of husbandry. The Renaissance Italian looked on nature with suspicion unless it had been tamed by man. If the site is, in Palladio's words, a theatre, the Rotonda is an actor of sorts, elegantly strutting its role on a podium, costumed in the paraphernalia of a glorious past.

This role was to have been still more grandly performed at the Trissino villa in Meledo, Palladio's only other hilltop site, where *belvedere* and farm were to join in an imposing crescendo that became the model for centuries of architectural pomp. Only a piece of one wing was executed, but the little woodcut of the project in the *Quattro Libri* [35] was enough to assure it a far greater role in the history of architecture than most completed buildings have played. What gives the composition its commanding character is that the hieratic system is enhanced in a new spatial dimension: upward as well as back and to the centre. Palladio used not only the rise in the land to elevate this building, but also a huge masonry substructure to create a sequence of platforms. Somehow we irrational humans are impressed by merely having to exert effort to get an experience. I believe

30. Villa Sarego, completed half of court

that the idea of using this kind of ascent for architectural effect was suggested by Roman models, and above all by the sanctuary of Fortuna at Praeneste, which Palladio drew in many fanciful reconstructions, one of which [94] has the same domed tempietto with porches on four sides.

The Meledo villa draws attention to Palladio's unique use of external stairs. Interior stairways in Palladio's villas are usually tucked into the un-lit leftover space on either side of the central tract, and never become an important expressive element of the interior as they do in many eighteenth-century Palladian houses. Palladio explains this in discussing Villa Poiana, where the uppermost storey is reserved for grain storage and the lower for kitchens and other storerooms, so that the internal stairs are rarely used by the owners. This gives the external stairs, which lead directly to the *piano nobile*, a design function greater than in any previous domestic architecture.

No wonder Meledo remained unfinished; it was not the house for a provincial gentleman but rather for a duke or a pope; Vasari called it a palace with villa functions. The same is true of the grandiose projects for Leonardo Mocenigo on the banks of the Brenta and for the Thiene family at Quinto [37], where the simple accumulation of elements to-ward a climax has been made more complex and subtle by the creation of three separate units. This is the scale on which Palladio visualized and reconstructed the Roman house [38]. It is characteristic of his view of antiquity that he represented it mostly in terms of buildings of super-human grandeur. Inevitably, perhaps, since the ordinary Roman house had not been excavated in his day. He saw things in Imperial scale, though with some exceptions he was practical enough to get his projects built for patrons of modest means.

What is it about Palladio's villas that made them so popular throughout the ensuing centuries, each of which has created a Palladian style ? Politics and religion helped : Palladio was more appreciated in the Protestant north

31. Villa Rotonda

32. Villa Rotonda, plan

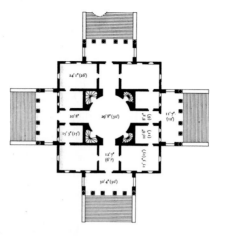

33. Villa Rotonda, view from below

and Michelangelo more in the Catholic Mediterranean, and as northern culture became dominant in the Europe of absolutist states and scientific revolution, the Palladian trend spread. Northerners like the cerebral, abstract quality in Palladio; besides, they could get at him through his *Quattro Libri*, without travelling to Italy, much less to the inaccessible backwaters of the Veneto. Without that remarkable monument of public relations, there could have been no Palladianism. The success of Palladio's book was in fact made possible by the abstractness of his style; a designer who thinks in terms of proportions in the plane can communicate the essence of his concepts in line. A book of woodcuts of the work of Michelangelo or Bernini would have misrepresented them grossly, and could not have excited a following even among audiences attuned to their expressionist effects.

But the Palladian vogues were motivated by more than Protestant culture and the accessibility of books. Palladio's clients were country gentry in much the same way that British squires and American plantation owners were. The country landowner in eighteenth-century Anglo-Saxon culture, like his predecessor in the Veneto of the sixteenth century, was economically tied to the land as overseer of the crops and the herds, but a classical education and the ambitions of a Humanist gave him city tastes. Seeking models for his dwelling, he would not have been attracted to the scenic Tuscan or Roman villa with its cypresses and formal parterres; northern weather and an agrarian economy did not encourage vast ornamental landscaping schemes in which the utility structures were pushed into the background by pools and fountains. He preferred the Palladian Villa, designed for an economic and social situation nearly identical to his own.

Thus Inigo Jones, England's first architect of international stature, sought out Palladio's follower Scamozzi, in the early seventeenth century, and began to direct the Palladian stream northward. In the eighteenth

34. Villa Rotonda, interior of cupola

century, Lord Burlington, who acquired the drawings of Palladio, built his country seat, Chiswick, on a Rotonda-like model – it was also a sort of *belvedere* rather than a functioning villa – while the plantation owners of Virginia raised Georgian elevations on Palladian plans. President Jefferson made the University of Virginia into an extended Villa Meledo, and his project for the house of the president of the United States, all too literally stolen from illustrations of the Villa Rotonda, was luckily rejected.

But even after the Industrial Revolution had forced the squire off the land, features of Palladian design survived: the triadic symmetry, axial planning, the search for harmonic proportions, the classic purity of the block and supporting members. This would not have surprised Palladio, who believed that his principles of design derived from eternally valid natural laws. But the longevity of Palladianism is not due so much to a discovery of the secrets of nature as to the persistence in our European-American culture of Renaissance ideals: for all our so-called 'revolutions' in recent art, we are much closer to Palladio than he was to the Middle Ages or even, in a sense, to antiquity.

35. Meledo, Villa Trissino, plan and elevation

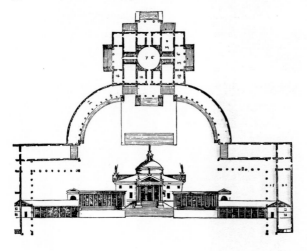

3: Civic and Domestic Architecture

Most studies of Palladio's work are typological. They treat villas, palaces, and churches separately, not just to simplify criticism, but to stress real differences in the social, economic and aesthetic roots of Palladio's designs. For instance, nearly all his ecclesiastical work was done for and in central cities, especially Venice, while all his palaces and civic structures were built in Vicenza [39] and other small towns in the Veneto and Friuli. Apart from a drawing that appears to be for a Grand Canal façade [62], Palladio left only one secular project for Venice (*Quattro Libri*, 11, 72), and that was never built. The Venetians, being less zealous about antiquity and classical harmony than the provincials, may not have wanted Palladian palaces; in any case, they were more alert than the mainlanders to signs of financial instability, and did not start palaces after 1560. They were right to be wary; not one of Palladio's private patrons finished more than half a palace, and only one of his public buildings was completed.

Since Palladio's patrons wanted a palace to be a public affirmation of their Humanist faith as well as of their wealth and status, most of them did manage to finish the façade and entrance way, if nothing else. Vicenza has about ten Palladio façades with barely enough original rooms behind them to furnish two dwellings. Yet those ten, mostly grand in scale, radically changed the atmosphere of sixteenth-century Vicenza, where no major dwelling of a real Renaissance character had existed before Palladio [39]. It was like the outburst of palace building in Florence in 1445-90, only it came too late, and the *signori* lacked the power they were so eager to symbolize.

Vicenza was not a partner of Venice, but a tributary. Her administrative and judicial lords were Venetian noblemen sent out for two-year terms by the Serenissima, as the Republic called itself, and no Vicentine ever gained admission to the closed society of the Venetian governing aristocracy. While some may have aspired to this distinction, the majority were

36. Villa Thiene, the sole completed pavilion

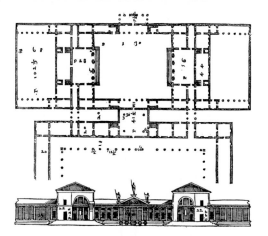

37. Villa Thiene, plan and elevation

resentful, and anyhow they were attracted to the Holy Roman Empire as the source of their titles to aristocracy. In the fourteenth century, the Scaligers of Verona and the Visconti of Lombardy ruled as vicars of the Emperor, until Vicenza was forced in 1404 to request the protection of Venice. This made Vicenza the butt of the power struggles of the early sixteenth century. When the Pope and the Emperor joined to crush Venice in the war of 1509–17, Vicenza, then a town of about 20,000 inhabitants, was at the centre of the battle ground, and the decision of the council of nobles to rejoin the Empire permitted both sides to call Vicenza traitorous and to sack and rob the city in turn for a decade. War and plagues, followed by a time of slow recovery and uncertain peace until the 1530s, disrupted the arts. Vicenza missed the flowering of the Renaissance, and the older tradition had been broken; hardly any major buildings could be raised in the first four decades of the century. Thus Palladio matured at the crucial moment, and he had to restore an art that had lost its continuity. This partly explains his voracious assimilation of the inventions of Roman and other north Italian architects in his early years.

In the contemporary histories of Barbarano and Marzari, members of the noble families for whom Palladio worked – the Chiericati, Trissino,

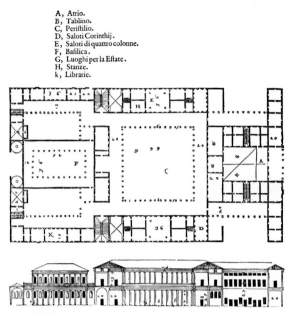

A, Atrio.
B, Tablino.
C, Periftilio.
D, Saloti Corinthij.
E, Saloti di quattro colonne.
F, Bafilica.
G, Luoghi per la Eftate.
H, Stanze.
k, Librarie.

38. Palladio's version of the Roman House

Thiene, Porto and others – appear predominately as *condottieri* and military specialists, though a small number appear as jurists or litterati, and one, Gaetano da Thiene, founded the Theatine Order and was canonized. They fought for a living, often for the Emperor or the King of France or Duke of Savoy, but also for Venice. They distinguished themselves in the victory of Lepanto over the Turks in 1571, which is commemorated by Palladio's Loggia [67]. They also fought each other in the streets of Vicenza. The chronicles are so filled with vendettas and murders by, and of, the nobility as to prompt a suspicion that the Humanistic culture professed by some of the members of the Accademia Olimpica and Accademia dei Costanti was only a thin veneer.

Vicenza was also a vanguard of the Protestant reform in north Italy. It was close to Germany, it had a large northern population, and its miseries

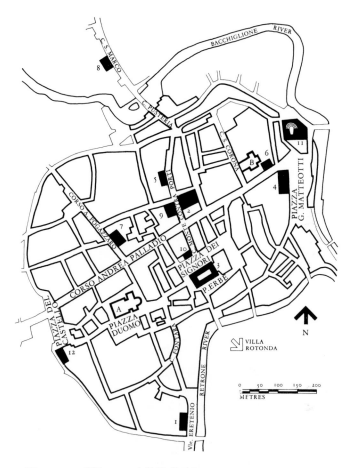

39. The centre of Vicenza: A Palladio itinerary

1. Casa Civena, after 1540
2. Palazzo Thiene, after 1542
3. Basilica, 1549
4. Palazzo Chiericati, 1550
5. Palazzo Iseppo Porto, late 1540s
6. Casa Cogollo, 1559?-67*
7. Palazzo Valmarana, 1565-6

8. Palazzo Schio-Angaran, before 1566
9. Palazzo Barbarano, before 1570-71
10. Loggia del Capitaniato, 1571
11. Teatro Olimpico, 1580
12. Palazzo Porto-Breganze, 1570s
A. Cathedral (apse, vault, 1565)
B. Sta Corona (Valmarana Chapel, 1576)

*The attribution of Casa Cogollo is contested. In my opinion it is not by Palladio.

40. Basilica, from Piazza dei Signori

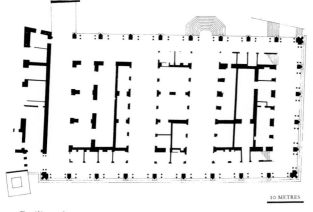

10 METRES

41. Basilica, plan

promoted sympathy for the earnestness and purity of the Lutheran Articles. Partly for this reason, Pope Paul III called a Council in Vicenza in 1538, but prematurely; political pressures deferred it over eight years, and forced its removal to Trent.

A picture of Palladio's environment as Imperial, military and reforming would be distorted, though it emphasizes ways in which Vicenza was exceptional. Many nobles, and nearly all the middle and lower classes, preferred Venice and peace and called themselves Catholic. But if Palladio's patrons were unsophisticated soldiers, they aspired to an air of ancient grandeur and an affiliation with northern Europe, and they shared a culture quite different from that of Michelangelo's and Vasari's patrons, or even from the Venetian aristocracy of their time. No wonder Palladio's architecture was unique.

Palladio's first public commission was to construct a two-storey loggia round the Palazzo della Ragione, the great meeting hall of Vicenza's Council of the Five Hundred referred to since his time as the Basilica ([40–43]; designed 1546–49, under construction until 1617). Its reputation as Palladio's outstanding and characteristic design is due to its size,

42. Basilica, northwest corner

43. Basilica, upper gallery

elegance and favoured position on Vicenza's major square rather than to a just assessment of its significance.

The vast, wooden-roofed, Gothic hall and the ground-floor network of vaults that support it were built in the mid-Quattrocento, partly on shops and storerooms of earlier centuries, and were enveloped later in the century by a two-storey loggia that collapsed shortly after being finished. The wars of the following years forestalled reconstruction, but in the period 1538–42 the Council called the most distinguished architects in north Italy for a succession of consultations on the problems of structure and form: Sansovino, Serlio, Sanmicheli and Giulio Romano. Giulio's recommendation in 1542 that the old form be kept but reinforced was rejected by a council in which there was more passion for antiquity than for economy or tradition. The impasse led to the appointment of Palladio, a designer of only local reputation whose classical education and influential protectors must have recommended him more than his executed designs. But this took time. The Council, after requesting that one bay of the project submitted by Palladio in 1546 with his master Giovanni da Pedemuro be built in wood as a trial, deferred its decision. In 1548, new drawings were accepted, and were developed into a final model at the start of 1549.

Palladio's structure cannot be called a building; it was a screen around an existing building that functioned first as a buttressing system and second as an elegant and expressive piazza decoration ingeniously disguising the irregular trapezoidal plan [41] and the old-fashioned façade of the earlier core. Not only the urbanistic character, but much of the actual form was predetermined by the early palace: the height of the two storeys, the width and number of the bays, the heavy piers at the angles. Palladio's piers probably all envelop the surviving supports of the early arcade, and much of the vaulting in the lower corridor appears to have been retained from the late Quattrocento structure. So Palladio's only problem was to find an effective way of filling in two superimposed rows of rectangles of predetermined dimensions. That was not as simple as it sounds : the almost-square rectangles were not invented to suit the dimensions of a proper classical order, and they were all different widths. Since each of Palladio's bays had to have an arch of the same size, he needed elements (the pilasters engaged to the sides of the piers) that could be expanded or contracted according to the relative width or narrowness of any bay. The arbitrary spacing of the piers also affected the frieze ; many of the triglyphs and metopes had to be squeezed or shaved down, but it was done so skilfully that it is more noticeable in the plates of the *Quattro Libri* than in the Basilica itself.

The narrowing of the end bays [41, 42], the most obvious adjustment to the earlier structure, was a result of the heaviness of the angle piers, which support more vaulting than the others, the aisles of unequal width that meet behind, and the oblique angle of the corner. In these bays, the open oculi in the spandrels are suppressed, and the corner pier with a single engaged column hides the irregularity of the two façades by completely covering the angle. Only the north-west corner, where two sides of the arcade are visible at once, offered all these difficulties. Adjacent structures obstruct a view of the other three corners. Another optical refinement is shown in [43] : the columnar order of the upper gallery leans out, reflecting the Quattrocento wall opposite, which inclines inward for structural reasons. Maybe this was done to make the small order more visible from the piazza below. The façade itself is quite plumb.

Palladio used the arch-lintel combination of the bays so effectively that it came to be called the Palladian motif, although it had been invented by Bramante and popularized by Serlio. It may have been suggested to him by Sansovino's new Library, which had been started in 1537 and was still in construction when he visited Venice in 1548 [4]. The Library also influenced the Basilica by its exciting manipulation of light and shadow through the multiplication of apertures (arches, oculi, balustrades on two levels) and of silhouetted statues over each pier. None of these features appears in Palladio's early Basilica studies, which apparently preceded the Venice trip. Palladio could profit from Sansovino's failure as well as his inventiveness: the collapse of the Library arcade in 1545, which led to the architect's imprisonment, was a vivid lesson in the statics of this kind of system.

At this moment in his career, Palladio did not follow Sansovino's lead in covering surfaces with relief; he wanted the more Serlian contrast of extremes: black shadow against flat neutral walls. The stone is less white and hard than the Istrian kind used throughout Venice; it came from near-by Piovene, and it weathers with less contrast between exposed and pro-tected parts. The Basilica is Palladio's only work entirely in stone, and this partly explains why the construction dragged on until 1617.

The Basilica plan that Palladio illustrated in the *Quattro Libri* is a fantasy, a unique instance of the publication of an ideal and impossible project for a building already constructed in another way. It eliminates the very diffi-culties that brought the design into being and without which it would not have been commissioned.

As a palace designer, Palladio was slow to become independent. While his rural and ecclesiastical buildings had to accommodate new and special social and economic conditions, his palaces served almost the same

44. Palace project

purposes as those of the earlier sixteenth century in other Italian cities. The early palace sketches, especially the façade elevations [44], are amateurish collections of motifs reminiscent of Falconetto, Serlio, and, at best, of Sanmicheli.

From this period of the early forties comes the design of Casa Civena in Vicenza ([39, No. 1; 45] close to Serlio VII, ch. xxv), the least assertive of Palladio's works. The façade, with an open arcade at street level, is a continuous screen without a central emphasis. Its open passages, connecting one house to the next along the street to give the pedestrian cover, are characteristic of the Vicentine and other terrafirma Venetian housing of the Middle Ages and later. In discussing urban planning (*Quattro Libri*, II, ii), Palladio speaks approvingly of this tradition, and recommends it to contemporaries:

> But if one wants to separate the place where people walk from that which serves for the passage of carts and beasts, I should like to see the streets so divided that on either side porticoes be built along which the citizens might pass under cover to do their shopping without being bothered by sun, rain or snow. Almost all the streets of Padua, that venerable city, noted for its University, are of this sort.

At the Casa Civena this ancient tradition is assimilated into a Roman Renaissance formula learned not from Rome but from faint reverberations in the work of the three architects working in the Veneto [1, 5].

45. Casa Civena

Casa Civena has so little in common with Palladio's next work, the Palazzo Thiene ([46–50]: only part of two wings, opposite and to the right of the main entrance block, are finished), that they could not be assigned to the same architect by appearance alone. Palazzo Thiene has no roots in the Vicentine or north Italian tradition; it is quite Roman, the fruit of Palladio's two-month stay in Rome in 1541, and of his attraction to the work of Giulio Romano in Mantua. The elevations, which are far more mature and commanding than other early Palladio designs, are wholly in Giulio's style. Nearly every feature can be found in Mantua at the Palazzo del Té, Palazzo Ducale or Giulio's own house: the vigorous rustication on two storeys, rubbly below and sharper above, contrasting with smooth courses at the level of the window lintels; the unfinished columns of the atrium, and the window-frames clamped to the surface by blocks, which are still closer to those of a small house in Rome [51, 48]. Because Palladio never copied another master so slavishly and because copies in general are rarely so full of vitality, some direct intervention by Giulio in the form of elevation sketches is conceivable. In 1542, he was in Vicenza as a Basilica consultant, two months after the signing of a contract for the construction of a residence for the Thiene – apparently the same palace. In the contract, Palladio still appears as a mason, which is an uncommon designation for a designer. Some shaky evidence for Giulio's participation comes from a note that Inigo Jones jotted into his copy of the *Quattro Libri* when he visited the palace in 1613; 'Scamozzi and Palermo said that these designs were of Julio Romano, but adjusted by Palladio, and so it seems.' Scamozzi, the executor of Palladio's architectural testament, must have known the truth, but in his hatred of his predecessor, which Jones mentions, he was capable of twisting it.

There are no data on the palace between the 1542 contract and the departure from Vicenza in 1553 of the sculptor Alessandro Vittoria, who decorated rooms on both storeys. Construction may have begun in the

46. Palazzo Thiene, east façade

mid 1540s and continued until the inscriptions were cut into the bands separating the storeys of the court on the East (in 1556) and North (in 1558). An unpublished map of Vicenza of about 1570 shows the east wing in its present state and the upper storey of the north wing incomplete.

The plan is Palladian in its symmetrical disposition of the four wings and the variously shaped rooms, but its Romanness appears in the huge court [47] that would have caused the Palace to fill an entire city block, and in the faint projection of vestigial towers at the four corners, which recalls the Cancelleria and Bramante's unfinished Palazzo dei Tribunali in Rome. The design of the principal façade, which was to face the main street of Vicenza [39, No. 2; 47] is uncertain. The whole front block seems to have been added as an afterthought onto a completed plan of the Palazzo del Té type. Besides, the plan in the *Quattro Libri* does not conform to the section or to the text, which says that a central 'loggia' is flanked by rows of shops – also a Roman feature, though Palladio specifically claims it as his own. Neither shops nor loggia appear in the plan,

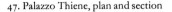

47. Palazzo Thiene, plan and section

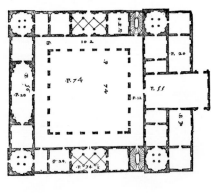

48. Palazzo Thiene, façade detail

but the latter, at least, can be reconstructed, as Bertotti Scamozzi thought, simply by making ample archways out of the three windows in the front wall of the centre block. The forward projection of this block is quite new, and makes an effective counterweight to the threatened monotony of the vast façade. It attracted imitators in the eighteenth and nineteenth centuries (Newgate Prison, London, designs by C. N. Ledoux). Another original and moving invention was not repeated later: the great court arcade of the *piano nobile* [49], which is taller than the ground floor arcade if the balconies are counted. It admits unimpeded light into the rooms behind, which are also illuminated from the street, and achieves a new kind of monumentality that was without ancient or modern precedent.

49. Palazzo Thiene, completed sections of the court

50. Palazzo Thiene, interior

51. Project for a house in Rome [Giulio Romano]

Palladio had little to do in the 1540s, but the Basilica commission of 1549 brought sudden success and a shower of palace commissions. His response to the first, for Girolamo Chiericati, one of the Basilica supervisors, was a rejection of the Roman Renaissance and a return to the Vicentine and Casa Civena solution of a block with its axis parallel to the pavement, which it envelops in a loggia, and no interior court [52, 53]. A new feature, the tripartite division, gives the block a determinate central focus and offers the alternatives of walking-along or walking-into. It is no longer a terrace house but a Renaissance monument that has to be looked at alone. And it did stand quite alone as the first palace alongside the big open 'Isola' which extended some 150 yards to the river bank [39, No. 4]. The covered passageway therefore lost its old function, and it never appears again in Palladio's palace designs. This kind of three-part façade cannot be effective without some open space before it, because its proportional relationships can be seen only at a distance and from a central position. It would not work in a narrow city street. So the Palazzo Chiericati and other urban projects for squares or broad streets could be treated more like villas than like the contemporaneous group of narrow-street projects. The Chiericati plan ([90] : discussed on pp. 164–7) is related closely to a number of villa studies of this period, not because Palladio wanted to suggest anything rustic, but because he was excited by the villa problem, and had found imaginative solutions for it.

A number of small city palaces of the 1550s illustrated in Palladio's book are indistinguishable from the compact sort of villa intended for village sites like Montagnana [20] or Piombino Dese [18]. They have central pedimented porticoes and very simple flanking wings (palaces for the Garzadore, Capra and Trissino families in Vicenza, and one of the two for Giovanni Battista della Torre in Verona, *Quattro Libri*, II, pp. 20, 73, 76, 77). The only executed example of the group is Palazzo Antonini in Udine [54] : here, an open space is on the left (where Palladio intended to add an

52. Palazzo Chiericati

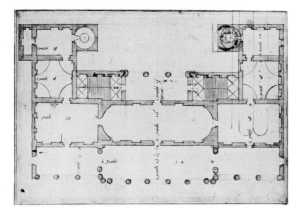

53. Palazzo Chiericati, original plan

asymmetrical kitchen) while the street is relatively narrow, so that the site suggested a more urban version of the villa-like palace façade with half columns on both floors that is effective when seen at an angle.

The 'urban' type was invented for narrow and deep plots facing narrow streets, and the bigger examples required a central court for light and air. The first, designed at about the same time as Palazzo Chiericati and finished in 1552, was for Iseppo Porto, brother-in-law of the builder of Palazzo Thiene. It was planned in what Palladio believed to be the ancient Roman style, with atrium entrances and a gigantic peristyle [39, No. 5; 55–7], while the elevations depended on modern designs Palladio had seen in his travels to Rome and elsewhere. The façade [55] was an interpretation of the house type of Bramante and Raphael ([3]: the two-storey-plus-attic elevation, the half columns, tall windows with alternating triangular and round pediments above and balustered balconies below), more mature than the Casa Civena, but flattened and sharpened in detail in the manner of Michele Sanmicheli at Palazzo Canossa in Verona of c.1530–40. The site precluded use of the carefully proportioned centring element of the 'villa' group, but the dull uniformity of Casa Civena is avoided by sculptural ornament in the central and end bays: Michelangelesque figures reclining on the pediment, and pendant garlands;

statues in the attic. All of Palladio's façades on such streets are variations of the Porto type in which horizontal emphases prevail over axial symmetry (Palazzos Thiene, Valmarana, Barbarano [46, 58, 63]). The plan, which is not revealed at all in the façade, is more original [56]. Identical building blocks for the family and for guests are placed on opposite sides of a court surrounded by a giant colonnade that supports a balcony at the *piano nobile* (later adapted to the Villa Sarego [30]). The three parts are not well knit, but the conception is fresh, and free from dependence on Venetian and central Italian precedent.

54. Palazzo Antonini, plan and elevation

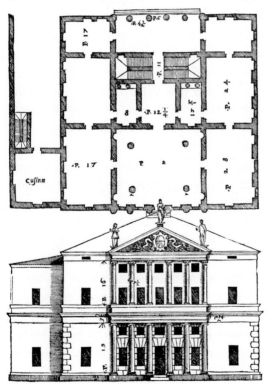

55. Palazzo Iseppo Porto

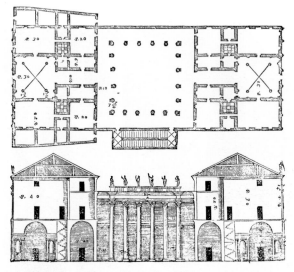

56. Palazzo Iseppo Porto, plan and section

In the decade starting in the mid fifties, when Palladio was overloaded with commissions for religious buildings and villas, he built no palaces that he felt worthy of inclusion in the *Quattro Libri*. This explains a break in continuity between the Palazzo Antonini in Udine [54] of 1556, which is a variation on the early tripartite type, and the Palazzo Valmarana in Vicenza [58–61] of 1565–6. The experience of these years, starting with a final trip to Rome in 1554, during the ascendancy of Michelangelo on the architectural scene there, and including the initial contacts with Venetian patronage and seascape, turned Palladio from the theoretical classicist of the preceding decade into a more encompassing and sensitive designer who surpassed proportion and Vitruvian *Decorum* to attain a profound and sensuous style. His last archaeological design was the court of the Carità monastery [87, 88] of 1561. After this, he became a pictorial architect, seeking a richness of effect in the modulation of light and shade, a

58. Palazzo Valmarana

texture of surface and a variety of colour that give the buildings of the last decade the character of late Imperial Roman architecture.

This change follows the decline of Palladio's engagement with the Roman Renaissance palace style of Bramante. Palazzo Valmarana is of a different sensibility; it has been called Mannerist, which helps to draw attention to unclassical features of its façade but invites the danger of drawing Palladio into an orbit that was foreign to him. The plan [59] cannot be given any style label because it grew out of specifically Palladian preoccupations and is unique. It retreats in the face of the practical demands of life and of irregular city sites from the excessive symmetry and ancient-Romanness of early designs. It is the soundest of the palace plans and the simplest, in that almost nothing is added just for visual or symbolic effect, such as the colossal peristyle of [56], and the forward half, which is all that was finished, still functions efficiently today after a sympathetic restoration, in part as the headquarters of Palladian research.

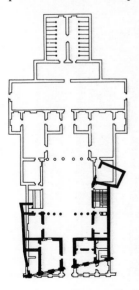

59. Palazzo Valmarana, plan (in black), compared to Palladio's project

60. Palazzo Valmarana, façade detail

61. Palazzo Valmarana, original elevation of façade and court

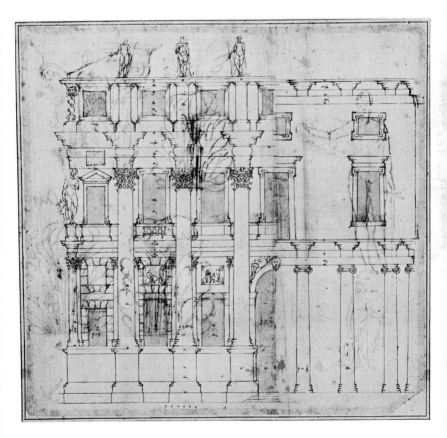

The much-discussed façade [39, No. 7; 58, 60, 61] is Palladio's most effective response to the narrow streets of Vicenza, because it was conceived in planes rather than in quasi-sculptural terms, and because the differentiated outer bays bridge the passage between the monumental central ones and the neutral façades on either side. The giant pilasters, being planar, help the integration with these neighbouring façades; they must have been suggested by Michelangelo's St Peter's model, which in 1547 introduced Rome to a new mode of architectural discourse in which ancient orders were used not merely symbolically but expressively, as affective forces (Michelangelo's Conservatori palace, begun in 1563, was still closer, but Palladio may not have seen drawings of it). The abrupt shift of scale in the end bays [58, 61], where the giant order is abandoned and all the apertures are altered, is carried out with an irony learned from Mannerists like Giulio, who liked to play architectural jokes on the purists. Still, it is like the classical solution for the Porto façade [55], where the end bays are differentiated by added ornamentation. The drawings for both façades have statues on the skyline over all but the end pilasters. The contemporaneous design of the façade of San Giorgio in Venice [86] solved the sudden shift in scale from a major order at the centre to a minor one at the outer edge in a similar way. In the palace, as in the church, the change in the outer bays is suggested by the plan; it corresponds to the more restricted dimensions of the interior spaces behind these bays.

Palladio was unfortunate in his last Vicentine commissions; not only were they not finished, but projects for the Palazzo Barbarano and the Loggia had to be altered hurriedly at the last minute, and the two lonely bays of the Palazzo Porto-Breganze and the proscenium of the Teatro Olimpico were built posthumously by the unsympathetic Scamozzi. Yet a rich and wholly novel late style emerged, in which the vocabulary of antiquity was used with dramatic freedom. Palladio abruptly abandoned

62. Palace project

the plane-and-pilaster formula of Palazzo Valmarana in favour of massive orders and balconies that project from walls consumed by relief sculpture and rugged textures. Geometry gave way to the changing contours and patterns of a pictorial vision.

An unexecuted project for a grandiose palace façade on a waterfront site of around 1570 or later also reveals the new spirit [62]. Probably it was designed for Venice rather than for the Vicenza river bank because it is Palladio's only palace that follows the medieval Venetian tradition of façades with broad central sections filled with tightly spaced windows required to light the deep halls and *saloni* that extend from the front to the rear [15]. Palladio eliminates sculpture here because the architectural elements themselves are sculptural enough, and seem especially so on the upper storey, where the wall area is so reduced that the triple central window looks incapable of supporting the stresses upon it. There is a fine balance of the familiar – the rustication of the lower storeys – and the radical – the giant half-columns and vigorously robust balconies – in a façade that would have reigned splendidly over the Grand Canal.

Palazzo Montano Barbarano (or Porto-Barbarano, [39, No. 9; 63, 64]) was designed in 1570 at the start of a financial crisis that halted construction on all Palladio's palaces. Even its aristocratic owner had difficulty

63. Palazzo Barbarano

64. Palazzo Barbarano, façade detail

65. Palazzo Porto-Breganze

in buying a proper building site, and proceeded with an irregular one invaded by earlier buildings on the left of the court. Palladio's first plan with its long atrium and court in the central tract – reminiscent of the Venetian tradition and of Sanmicheli's Veronese palaces – also developed naturally from his own earlier innovations. Almost nothing of it is preserved except the ample atrium which, in spite of its irregular form, has an imposing harmony that rings through its present decay. Palladio wrote that the plan already had been altered at the time of publication of the *Quattro Libri*, but too late to allow the preparation of a new cut; maybe the client had acquired the missing piece of property. The existing plan is so disorderly, however, that it must represent a major departure from Palladio's revised project. Some time in the later sixteenth century (?) two extra bays were added to the façade, throwing the portal off-centre. The rectangular reliefs on the ground floor were interpolated also, in imitation of the Palazzo Valmarana [64]. Palladio wrote that he changed the façade when he changed the plan, but does not say why; the first scheme with a giant order, shown in a small cut in the *Quattro Libri*, was abandoned in favour of superimposed half-columns to achieve a pictorial enrichment of the early formula of the Palazzo Iseppo Porto [55]. Probably he calculated that the giant order would be too dramatic for the narrow street; in substituting the present design he adjusted the façade to the scale of the site by making the lower order equal to the width of the street.

Where giant half-columns were used, as at the Loggia del Capitaniato [39, No. 10; 66] and the Palazzo Porto-Breganze [39, No. 12; 65], ample squares offered distant and varied viewpoints; the church façades, where Palladio developed his taste for this motive, were also unencumbered; in fact, the order of the Porto Palace [65], with its high podia and its swags between the capitals, is almost a replica of that on the San Giorgio façade [86]. How were the lonely two bays of this building to have grown into a proper palace? Vincenzo Scamozzi, who supervised the construction, wrote in his *Idea della architettura universale* of 1615 only that the palace was among those that he had 'finished . . . but with certain changes' (he was too envious to mention Palladio in any of his writings). The portion completed is only one room wide and extends into a rear court with one-storey half columns along the wall, the last of which faintly indicates the beginning of a curved rear wall that Bertotti Scamozzi, in his plates of 1776, restored persuasively as a theatre-like hemicycle, a novel idea that probably was Palladio's. Bertotti drew the hemicycle as high as the façade, which would have made the court a dark well; a one-storey elevation of the type of Palazzo Pitti in Florence would be more convincing.

The partly finished Loggia del Capitaniato in the Piazza dei Signori in [Vicenza 66–8] of 1571–2, poses the same problem. It appears from the

66. Loggia del Capitaniato, view from Basilica

67. Loggia del Capitaniato, east side

unexecuted façade on the left side [cf. 39, No. 10] that Palladio meant to extend it farther, perhaps to five bays (the seven-bay elevation proposed by Bertotti and other early critics is oversized and counter to the tradition of civic loggias). But already in 1572, financial pressures forced a compromise on the present form. Thus the inscription celebrating the generosity of the Venetian Captain who helped the city raise this elegant addition to his palace: IO(HANNI) BAPTISTAE BERNARDO PRAEFECTO CIVITAS DICAVIT starts at the left of the frieze, implying no further expansion, and continues around the building. Palladio may have left a five-bay model. In a contract of 1671 for the demolition of an adjoining house and the extension of the loggia there are frequent references to an existing model, and it could have survived a century.

Nearly every Italian commune had an open, arched loggia in its main square from the early Middle Ages on that served as a revered symbol of communal justice and government and as a stage for civic ceremony. Some were simply vaulted canopies, like the Loggia dei Priori (Lanzi) in Florence or Sansovino's loggia in St Mark's Square in Venice, but more often (as in Milan, Brescia, Verona, Pistoia and Vicenza) the arcade carried a *piano nobile* which served either as a meeting hall or a residence for the chief magistrate. The medieval loggia in Vicenza was destroyed, probably as the symbol of Venetian rule, by Imperial troops during the wars of the second decade of the sixteenth century, and in 1521 the city replaced it with one designed by the Venetian architect Scarpagnino. In 1565, the *maggior consiglio* passed an appropriation to buy property around it and the adjacent Captain's palace in order to make another loggia with a meeting hall above for its own deliberations. Not until April 1571, when the loggia threatened to collapse, was a committee formed to advise on whether it should be repaired or replaced. The latter alternative was recommended at once and work proceeded so rapidly that part of the new structure was under cover by November of the same year. The speed was

68. Loggia del Capitaniato, façade detail

incredible, considering that the Basilica was in construction for sixty-eight years. Had the design been prepared in 1565 so that work could begin without time-consuming negotiations with the architect in Venice? Or was the new loggia raised on the foundations of the old with the aid of its materials? An inscription on the side façade, ANDREA PALLADIO I(nvenit?) ARCHIT, identifies the designer, who spent hardly any time in Vicenza during the construction and, having lost two sons in the course of the year, refused the city's pleas to come during the last months of construction.

The original Palladio design of the side façade underwent a sudden change in October of 1571 [67], when the Turks were defeated at the crucial battle of Lepanto with the help of two battleships from Vicenza and a huge financial assessment that forced the loggia commissioners to abandon the hope of completing the original project. The lateral façade became a triumphal arch with statues of Peace (as Vicenza) and Victory (as Venice) on the lower storey and a field for trophies and allegories of civic virtues above. The one-storey columnar order and the shift in scale and focus from the piazza façade [66] causes a discontinuity that seems to have come from the sudden change in plan; but as the architecture was so nearly finished at this point, it may be that Palladio intended the effect from the start; its failure to work visually can be attributed to Palladio's absence from the site, the speed of construction, and the excess of sculpture imposed by the triumphal programme. But these reasons have been used too highhandedly to explain any element that critics have found unfamiliar, such as the breaking of the entablature by the window frames, a motive that did not disturb Palladio, who used it in the façade project of [62].

Military trophies also fill the entire wall surface of the piazza façade, referring rather to the protective role of the Capitano than to Lepanto. Inside, there were frescoes by Veronese's follower Fasolo, with the stories of three self-sacrificing Roman leaders, which indicate that the Captain, not the council, occupied the hall.

This building, so Roman in its triumphal iconography, turns from Vitruvian purism toward Imperial models like the triumphal arch of Septimius Severus in the Roman forum, which may have suggested the broken surfaces and the entablature that projects forward over the columns. The colourism (the brick surfaces of the columns were not meant to be stuccoed over), the windows that interrupt the architrave, and the robust triglyph-supports of the balconies are examples of the unclassical spirit of Palladio's last years.

Not one of Palladio's palace courts is as much as half completed, so that we lack a sense of the scale and of the quality of the environments he envisioned. Of the small number of original rooms surviving, the majority are on the ground floor, and we know almost nothing of projects for the *piani nobili*. They are not illustrated in the *Quattro Libri* nor recorded among the surviving sketches. In most cases Palladio must have assumed that they would correspond more or less to the plan below, with the *salone* resting on the atrium vault (the one fully preserved *piano nobile* – at Palazzo Antonini in Udine – does just this [54]) and he indicates only whether the rooms are to be vaulted or beamed. This repetition is a radical departure from earlier palace design elsewhere in Italy, where the ground floor was given over to shops, kitchens, storerooms and other mundane functions, leaving elegance, proportion and spaciousness to dwelling and reception rooms above. That Palladio meant to eliminate such functional differences between the two storeys is suggested not only by the equivalence in plan, but by the decorations lavished on street-level rooms, notably in the Chiericati and Thiene palaces. His motivation was intellectual and not social. Besides preferring the structural and formal logic of putting all the upper walls on corresponding lower walls, he wanted to revive aspects of the ancient Roman house, where the principal family activities took place on the ground – often the only – floor. He cannot have succeeded in this way in changing his client's way of life. The dark, damp and cold of the rooms below probably kept the Cinquecento inhabitants, like their modern successors, upstairs.

Where the internal decoration is preserved, it complements the architecture, and the scrupulousness with which Palladio credits, in the *Quattro Libri*, the work of sculptors, stuccoists and fresco painters who worked in each building implies a collaborative effort – probably initiated after the construction, since the ornament is never structural and usually occupies only the vaults. In most cases, the sculpture and relief is in the manner of Alessandro Vittoria and his circle, if not actually by that group [50]. The painting also is characteristic of Venetian Mannerism. Consequently the style is not really a decorative equivalent to Palladio's architecture in the sense that Veronese's frescoes at Maser are [9] but heavier and denser, less clear in spatial character, and incapable of leaving the smallest surface untouched.

The façade sculptures are slightly more sympathetic to the architecture because more of them were executed under Palladio's supervision, yet the ornament shown in his drawings and woodcuts is simpler and larger in conception than on the actual buildings. The decorations of Palazzo Barbarano [64] are fussier than Palladio intended; sculptors added the crowded frieze, which Palladio shows as the unadorned pulvinated (or cushion) type, and effulgent Manneristic cartouches over each window of the lower order. Excessive detail and loss of bold scale also weaken the stuccoes of the Loggia del Capitaniato [66, 67]. Even in an early façade like Palazzo Iseppo Porto [55], which Palladio surely supervised carefully, the masks over the pediments, the billowing scarves of the figures and the complexity of the hanging garlands are absent from the drawing. The iconography escaped Palladio's control, too: the military triumphs in the relief panels of Palazzo Valmarana [60] replace what appear to be allegories in the drawing [61], though the two statues in the end bays are, as intended, Roman soldiers. Probably the patrons dealt directly with the decorators after Palladio's departure. These changes sapped the tectonic vigour of Palladio's buildings. In his drawings, he never let sculpture diminish the force of architectural discourse but enclosed it within a frame, supported it on or suspended it from an architectural element, so that it should remain subordinate. This was classical practice, consciously opposed to the over-all relief effects of some central Italian Mannerist façades.

4: Ecclesiastical Architecture

When Palladio began to build churches he was over fifty and had already designed most of his palaces and villas; there are no church projects among his early drawings. Scarcity of patronage was the reason, rather than lack of religious sentiment: Palladio's books show him to have been more pious than most Humanists. His contemporaries in the Veneto were not irreligious, either, though many of them were anti-Papists. The Church had instigated a devastating war against the Republic in 1509 with an interdict, and the Protestant Reformation got a hospitable welcome in this channel to northern Europe which had always been independent in religious as well as in political affairs. Major commissions, then, were as likely to be supported by civic or private as by ecclesiastical funds, and these, partly because of the wars, were sparse before the mid sixteenth century.

Palladio wrote of church architecture as glorifying God and embellishing the city; he ignored the institution of the Church. Several of his major ecclesiastical commissions were civic or private (project for Brescia Cathedral; the Redentore in Venice; the façade of San Petronio in Bologna; the villa-chapel at Maser), and most of the others were monastic (Monastery of the Carità; San Giorgio Maggiore; San Nicola da Tolentino, all in Venice). Yet, differences in the sources of funds do not seem to have affected the character of the designs. Until recently, for example, drawings for San Nicola were thought to be studies for Maser. The different types were experiments in the search for a modern civic 'temple' that Palladio believed should surpass its ancient ancestor in beauty and dignity as much as the Christian faith surpassed what he called 'their vain and false superstition'.

His hope of surpassing antiquity indicates a new viewpoint, expressed at the same time by Michelangelo, which in time replaced the Humanists' ambition merely to equal or to imitate the achievements of the ancients. It anticipated the belief in cultural progress that pervaded early modern thought. As church builders, both Palladio and Michelangelo were creative Christians, moved by the crisis of the Reform – one in the separatist atmosphere of Venice, the other in the ambience of the Roman oratories – to reconsider the traditions of the church as a structure just as theologians of the time were re-examining the Church as an institution.

Church design of the early sixteenth century betrayed the institutional decay that prompted the Reformation. The Humanist architects of the Renaissance, from Alberti to Palladio himself (in his writings) had tried to establish the central plan church – preferably circular or square – as the dominant type, because it was 'the most beautiful and regular' (*Quattro Libri*, IV, ii). St Peter's in the Vatican was started on this principle, but throughout its history of over a century of construction (1506–1612), the architects and the Holy See vacillated between the original intention, longitudinal projects, and compromises between the two. The same uncertainty attended Palladio's initial project for the Redentore. The architect was asked to submit two models, 'one in round form and one in rectangular form'; apparently, the former was selected and then abandoned, after a vigorous dispute, just before construction was started.

But if the central plan church was desirable philosophically and visually, it was ill-suited to a liturgy and customs that had evolved over the centuries in churches with long naves. The clergymen who often defeated the schemes of Alberti, Bramante and others were not just conservatives who wanted to keep medieval forms, but practical professionals who foresaw the problems of placing members of the choir or of conducting services in a cylindrical space with an altar either in the middle or in a chapel off to one side. The architects, particularly the theorists, did not listen to them; they continued to spend their time and effort drawing central plans, while public opinion forced them to construct a larger number of longitudinal churches. Even really inventive longitudinal designs like Giulio Romano's San Benedetto Po and some of the St Peter's projects did not stimulate an evolution of the type during the first half of the sixteenth century. Most of the churches were dull in form and unimaginative in structure, like those of Antonio da Sangallo in Rome.

Outside Rome, church building lagged. In the Veneto, the constant state of war inhibited building in general. A major architect like Sanmichele, the author of many palaces and civic buildings, made only one (central plan) church. The other great pre-Palladian in the Veneto, Sansovino, participated in designing several churches in Venice itself, but none was built just as he intended, and none had the strength to promote significant departures from the vigorous local style of Coducci and Lombardi of the turn of the century.

Elsewhere in Italy, even otherwise competent architects produced indecisive church designs in the first half of the century; a change in architecture had to await changes in the Church as an institution. The Jesuits and other reforming movements, the Council of Trent, and the complex of attitudes we call the Counter-Reformation created a climate in which architectural imagination could be regenerated within rather than outside the church. During the 1560s Palladio and two outstanding contemporaries, Giacomo Barozzi da Vignola (1507–73) and Galeazzo Alessi (1512–72), realized a new kind of ecclesiastical space. Their achievement was to mend the break caused by the Humanist abandonment of the traditional basilical form. They found ways to combine an ample nave for a large congregation and side chapels big enough for the celebration of the sacraments with the majestic domed central space that had been the testament of early Renaissance Tuscan architects to the St Peter's design of Bramante and Michelangelo. Earlier architects, trained as painters or sculptors, lacked the technical mastery with which these professionals solved the problems of supporting huge masonry domes without blocking or even restricting the passage from the nave or aisles into the crossing and of vaulting great spans to improve fire resistance and acoustics. And where preceding generations had tried to join disparate traditions by adding longitudinal naves to centralized crossings, the new designers really fused them into an entity.

That three architects in three major Italian cities created church plans during the 1560s similar in most of their radical features is an exceptional coincidence. Palladio's San Giorgio Maggiore, still an experiment in the new mode, is comparable to Alessi's San Vittore al Corpo in Milan (1560) and Vignola's unexecuted project for Santa Maria in Traspontina in Rome of 1565. All three designers rapidly developed mature schemes that were even more closely related. The Redentore [71], San Paolo e Barnaba in Milan of 1558, and the Gesù in Rome of 1570 [69] all have naves flanked by arches on piers, covered by barrel vaults, and brightly lit by thermal windows. The side chapels are joined by open passages, implying the fusion of aisle and chapel, and the crossing piers are drawn into the wall mass. The transept no longer projects far beyond the nave; both it and the crossing merge into a single upward- and outward-expanding space that is called in Italy a 'tribune'.

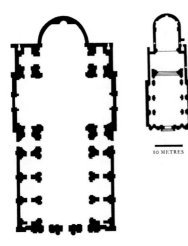

10 METRES

69. Il Gesù, San Barnaba; plans

129

These three architects were not brought so close by mutual contact but by common experience. Stimulated by the Council of Trent, artists as well as ecclesiastics began to think about the relations of the Church to its worshippers. The Council did not rule on architecture, but powerful theologians and prelates began to intervene with architects and patrons in formulating church programmes. The most effective of these was Cardinal Carlo Borromeo, whose *Instructiones Fabricae et Supellectilis Ecclesiasticae* of 1577 proposed a sort of reformed building and decorating code for church architects and decorators. He allowed some liberty in planning but explicitly favoured the Latin cross over central plans, and in a number of specific ways confirmed the direction taken by Alessi, Palladio and their contemporaries. The designs of San Giorgio and the Redentore reveal an earnest effort to find shapes for a rejuvenated liturgy: the elevation of the church on a podium, the care and inventiveness lavished on the choir, the separation of choir from chancel (a self-contained altar-house like San Giorgio's is unique in the Italian Renaissance), the almost complete abstention from non-architectural ornament, and, finally, the chaste whiteness of the whole interior.

The genesis of the Redentore design was bound more specifically to contemporary events. It was built by the Venetian Senate and delivered for care to the Capuchin Order in fulfilment of a vow on the deliverance of the city from the devastating plague of 1575-6. The Doge and Senators vowed to visit the church annually in perpetuity, and instituted a pompous cortège that passed over a temporary causeway thrown across the Giudecca canal and terminated in prayers within the tribune. Their legislation imposed on a single church three nearly autonomous ecclesiastic functions: monastic in the choir, votive in the tribune, and congregational in the nave and chapels (Palladio's initial proposal for a 'round' church may have had only a shallow narthex at the entrance instead of a nave). Thus the distinction of parts [70, 71]: the great tribune, from every

70. Il Redentore, section (from Bertotti Scamozzi)

angle in which the altar is visible so that a large company of dignitaries can follow the services from a privileged position, is clearly separated from the nave and side chapels by a pier that narrows the opening, and from the choir by a columnar screen through which light and sound can pass without compromising privacy [72]. The demand for separation must have reminded Palladio of his earlier intensive studies of the Imperial baths [92, 93], in which he had reconstructed sequences of independent spaces, sometimes visually connected through columnar screens like the one here. The Redentore nave is like the fanciful sketches of halls in the Baths of Agrippa behind the Pantheon in Rome. Palladio associated the problem of joining a rectangular nave to a central-plan tribune and a choir with that of linking thermal shapes and functions in a similar series: Frigidarium, Tepidarium and Calidarium.

The structure is Roman too. It discards the medieval tradition in which free-standing piers sustain vaults and domes in a fabric stabilized by delicately balanced stresses – a tradition that naturally accompanied the Latin cross church into the Renaissance. It meant the adoption of the Imperial Roman technique, already restored at St Peter's in the Vatican, of supporting vaulting by mouldable wall masses, penetrated by niches, on whose surface the classical columns serve a purely decorative function.

71. Il Redentore, plan

72. Il Redentore, nave, toward altar

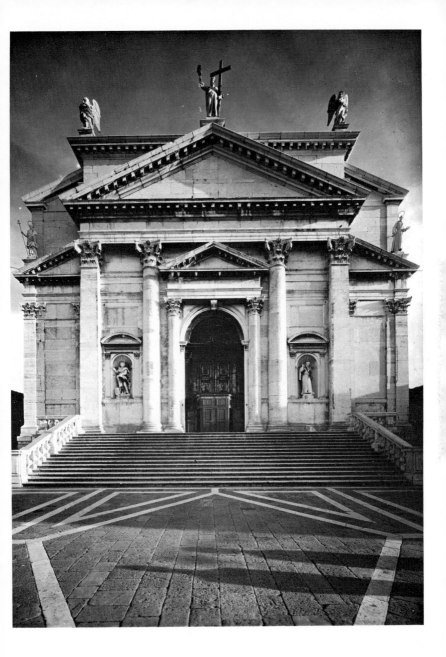

The design of the tempietto at Maser [75–7] was also motivated by the Roman conception of the wall as a plastic structural mass rather than a screen at the limits of a space. Here it facilitated the improbable union of two contrasting forms, the Greek cross and the domed Pantheon-with-portico, by permitting the dome to be supported and buttressed by wall masses that are invisible inside and deftly integrated into the exterior [76]. This union of perfect centrality with an entrance axis focusing attention on the altar solved the liturgical deficiency of earlier central plans and met Carlo Borromeo's demand for the cross symbolism. Yet the new solutions brought new problems: the wall mass inhibited fenestration, and the variety of spaces and of ornament is overbearing at so small a scale.

This irreverent child of the Pantheon is more Rococo than Roman. Its ornament is an innovation in Palladio's church design that first appeared in his later palaces: in profuse stucco relief that covers every surface of the interior cylinder [77] and outer pediment [75], it fragments light pictorially and pre-empts the clarity of surfaces with a sort of architectural impressionism antithetical to the Palladio of proportion and archaeology. Free-swinging swags between the porch capitals genially confuse shadow and substance. They frightened the neo-Classicists, but now they seem to be a natural outcome of the transfer of the classical vocabulary from stone to

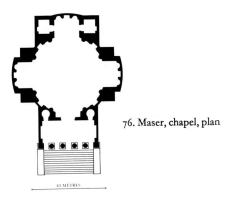

76. Maser, chapel, plan

10 METRES

terracotta and plaster – an architectural equivalent to the diffusion of colour and brush-stroke in the late works of Titian.

Had the chapel been published in the *Quattro Libri*, or had it been less inaccessible to the traveller, it might have made a deep impression on ecclesiastical architecture (the reappearance of the scheme in Mansart's Sainte Marie de la Visitation in Paris is probably due to harmony of spirit rather than to direct contact). Vignola's way of giving the central plan a dominant axis by stretching it into an oval proved to be more influential, being better attuned to Mannerist taste. Palladio and Vignola often set themselves similar problems and got similar answers: the incorporation of two towers in the façade of a central plan church, carried out for the first time (?) at Maser, was proposed independently in Vignola's preparatory drawings for the Gesù and projected for his unfinished façade of Sant'Anna dei Palafrenieri in the Vatican, of 1570. These towers appear also on the façade of the Zitelle church in Venice, near the Redentore on the Giudecca. It was completed posthumously in 1586, and the rest of the façade is so retrogressive from Palladio's later design that it is more likely to be the work of his associates and followers than an original of the last period. The interior, too, has been altered, as an eighteenth-century plan shows. The setting of the church between two wings of the convent is especially engaging, but characteristically Seicento.

Palladio's unexecuted projects recently identified with the Theatine church of San Nicola da Tolentino in Venice [78], in which an ample choir is added behind a columnar screen to the unified central space, are so much less mature than Maser, and less in harmony with other late works, that it is hard to credit the late date (1579) suggested by records of the acquisition of property by the Order.

An unresolved element in the earliest of Palladio's new churches was the façade. Façade design had bemused Italian architects since the Middle Ages – most Italian Gothic cathedrals have unfinished or modern fronts.

The problem was that the façade belonged more to the street or square than to the church itself, which needed nothing but a terminal wall with holes for doors and windows. The public function, and especially the opportunities for symbolism, demanded fine stonemasonry, which made the façade structurally as well as functionally separate from the inside. How could the architect make it look as if it belonged to the church behind as well as to the town ? And how could he pull together the tall nave and the low side-aisles alongside, particularly when he wanted to use ancient orders that had their own rules and could not be expanded and contracted at will ? How, finally, could the façade be given a spatial character consistent with the aesthetic of the Renaissance interior so as to avoid being a flat plane divided by horizontal and vertical strips ?

Palladio believed that none of these questions had been answered properly by his predecessors. He ignored the solutions that had been tried in Rome and Venice, and began anew. His first major ecclesiastical commission was the design of a façade for San Francesco della Vigna [79], a church that had already been completed more or less after designs

78. Project for San Nicola da Tolentino

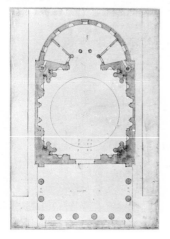

79. San Francesco della Vigna, façade

80. Project for the façade of San Petronio

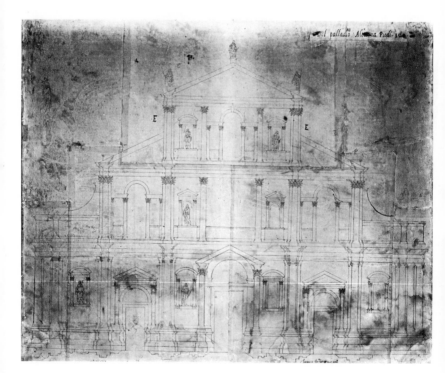

by Jacopo Sansovino. This characteristic division of labour precluded a serious integration of interior and façade. Sansovino's unexecuted façade, preserved in a medal, was too old-fashioned in the early 1560s, and Palladio simply applied his invention – the date is uncertain – as if the façade were an independent monument. He identified as the major issues in his design two problems that Sansovino had failed to solve: the integration of the high nave front with low side-chapel fronts, and the evocation of space within the confines of a nearly flat façade.

He found a solution in the columnar temple portico of antiquity with its crowning pediment, which he used on a grand scale in the centre and on a lesser scale in two halves on either side. To integrate centre and sides, he had to put a small and a giant order on the same base, which had not been done in ancient temples and led to contradictions: for example, the base on which the large and small orders rest could not look right for both; at San Francesco and in the late projects for San Petronio in Bologna [80] Palladio adjusted his bases to the former, and at San Giorgio Maggiore [86] he tried a compromise by starting the orders at different heights. The Redentore [74], where the stairs hid the trouble, represented an optimal solution of an essentially insoluble conflict.

The temple-front motive binds the sides to the centre by repeating similar triangular figures at smaller scale and by sustaining horizontal accents across the façade *behind* the giant order – more emphatically at San Giorgio than at San Francesco [86, 79]. To speak of a course as being behind an order is to introduce another innovation in Palladio's façades: the metaphor of space. The façade was designed as a relief, different layers of which should be revealed within the thickness of the wall; together with figures and columns, the wall-layers induce a chiaroscuro range from white to darkest shadow – a range intensified by the Istrian stone that bleaches in parts exposed to sun and rain and blackens in shadowy protected parts. But it is not only the relief treatment that implies depth;

anyone reading the temple-front historically sees it in part as a free-standing, open portico before a temple cella, or at least is aware that the simile is suggested. That Palladio had this interpretation in mind can be seen in a recently discovered plan of San Giorgio done in the mid 1570s, where he proposed to alter the original project, which had been enshrined in a model a decade before, by advancing the four central columns to create a *real* portico in three dimensions. If Palladio had lived to build a façade, it probably would have been this one; the present façade was executed after his model (of 1565) in 1607–10.

The base of the lateral half-pediments of the San Giorgio façade continues across the three central bays as a sort of cornice and appears to join the half-pediments into a single, low and broad, temple front behind the pseudo-portico at the centre. This probably was a gloss on the model by a later architect; in other works, Palladio did not specifically join the side pediments to one another because to do so would have misrepresented the church interior, and he meant the façade to introduce the scheme of the church. An early drawing for San Giorgio, presumably of 1565, has no binding motive of the sort, nor does San Francesco della Vigna [79], and in a letter of 1567 to the builders of Brescia Cathedral, Palladio spoke of the 'half-pediments' recommended for the side-aisle façades: since two halves together constitute all a single order can support, there could be no justification for a cornice between them.

The relationship of the smaller to the larger orders on the façade was meant to state something specific about the nature of the interior spaces: inside San Giorgio, as on the façade, the small pilasters of the side-aisles are based on the ground, and the giant half-columns on pedestals [84, 86]; at the Redentore, designed a decade later, the small and the giant order start at the same level, both inside and out [72, 74]; also the buttress system sustaining the Redentore vault is integrated into the façade design. These devices do not make a Palladio façade into a diagram of the church behind, but they do establish closer ties than one finds in contemporary churches elsewhere.

Called in 1572 to design a façade for the enormous Gothic church of San Petronio in Bologna, Palladio tried with only moderate success to incorporate a dull lower order applied earlier in the century; called again in 1578, he proposed to adapt the temple motives of the Venetian churches, first in designs related to the Redentore [80], and later by the addition of a vaulted forehall – called 'portico' in the correspondence – a drawing of which has just been discovered. The Cathedral chapter ultimately rejected the later designs because they required the destruction of all the existing Gothic and Renaissance work, but the decision could have been justified on aesthetic grounds, too. The scale of the order, greater than anything Roman, was excessive for the temple-reference, and the ratio of width to height overstretched Palladio's formula.

Though the façade design of 1558 for San Pietro in Castello in Venice was Palladio's first, it has not appeared here because the façade actually built by Smeraldi in 1596 cannot be the same; it does not conform to specifications in the 1558 contract, and it is a pastiche of Palladio's inventions in which elements like the Redentore buttresses lose the logic that brought them into being.

Palladio's façades deeply impressed later designers. Imitations appeared everywhere in Venice, and somewhere in every Western country for centuries after. This is due to more than a recognition of happy solutions to old dilemmas; it also testifies to the skilful exploitation of their pictorial role in the panorama of Venice. Few architects have been granted sites so splendidly endowed at once by nature and by a position in constant view of hordes of foreign visitors as well as Venetians. San Giorgio's façade is marvellously suited to its island eminence, where it is seen far oftener from a distance – from boats, the Piazzetta di San Marco and the Fondamenta alongside – than from nearby. But its pictorial effectiveness is a bit fortuitous; the most successful features – a giant order, brilliant stone, deep relief and sculptural detail – were invented for San Francesco della Vigna, which has only a small *campo* before it, and they just happened to work splendidly as a backdrop to the Canal scene. The stone façade of San Giorgio and its brick body were not conceived as a unit; seen from the direction of San Marco, the façade was meant to hide or to dominate the rest. The Redentore, on the other hand, must be understood as a more mature composition in which the dome, the towers, roof and buttresses are integrally bound to the façade [74]. Seen from directly across the Giudecca canal, the forward slope of the hipped roof flattens out to echo the main pediment; the buttresses appear to be not what they are, but auxiliary half-pediments; the dome and its flanking towers become repetitions of the tripartite temple-fronts. From this distant frontal position and from none other we grasp a proportional system; for example, the overall width of the façade is about the same as the height of the church to the base of the dome (83 as vs. 87 Vicentine feet according to a recent measured survey) and the height from the ground to the peak of the main pediment (68 1/3′) is half the overall height (137 5/6′).

As intellectual calculations of this kind work only in two dimensions, in a non-perspective sense, Palladio usually tried to manipulate the observer into an axial frontal position. In this case, frontality was assured by the distance across the canal, and an axial approach was assured by means which are apparent only once a year, on the feast of the Redeemer (third Sunday of July) when, in fulfilment of the vow of 1576, a causeway on barges is built across the water at a right angle to the façade. By contrast to a parish church to which the local populace comes from every direction, the Redentore has a pre-eminent function as the goal of a bridge-borne procession. The really important celebrants approach it full-on, as one approaches most of Palladio's villas along an allée, and see it almost the way one sees a woodcut elevation in the *Quattro Libri*. The impression of

81. San Giorgio Maggiore, view from cloister

two-dimensionality is sustained by the absence of chiaroscuro contrast; the façade looks toward the north and is never illuminated by direct sunlight.

If we need strictly frontal views to grasp the unity of the design, the Redentore and San Giorgio still look good at any angle [81]. The shapes and materials of the nave, tribune and dome are so simple and the sparsity of decorative detail so refreshing that the abrupt contrast to the façades is not disturbing. Unity is not always a virtue, and could not anyhow be a commitment in a building which combines, as the Redentore does, elements of the Roman temple and bath, the Byzantine dome and Gothic buttresses copied from San Petronio within a Humanist system of proportion.

San Giorgio belongs to a grand monastery that fills a large part of the Isola di San Giorgio at the end of the Giudecca [81]. Since the restoration

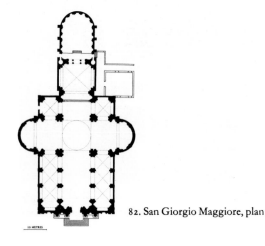

82. San Giorgio Maggiore, plan

83. San Giorgio Maggiore, refectory

85. San Giorgio Maggiore, transept

86. San Giorgio Maggiore, façade

of the whole complex by the Cini Foundation after the last war, it has become one of the major sights of Venice. Two large cloisters of similar dimensions, separated by a library wing, were projected early in the sixteenth century, but took a hundred years to build. The earlier, started in 1517 by Andrea Buora, is still Quattrocento in style; the latter, alongside the nave of the church, was redesigned by Palladio sometime before the adjoining buildings were begun in 1579, but was executed after his death and was not finished when Evelyn visited it in 1646. Modern critics have doubted Palladio's authorship because the proportions are pre-classical, recalling the Procuratie Vecchie in the Piazza di San Marco, but it is re-affirmed by a recently discovered plan of the church and cloister done in Palladio's shop during the 1570s. The master's intentions as shown there could have been altered only in details (one such detail was the addition of an open loggia-passage, probably by Longhena, in the centre of the wing between the two cloisters).

The Refectory, a noble barrel-vaulted hall approached up a grand ceremonial staircase and through an anteroom started in or before 1540, was completed by Palladio in 1560–2 [83]. The earlier construction fixed the proportions of the three areas and the placement and form of the windows (the early frames are preserved on the exterior), leaving Palladio free to design only the covering and details. Unfortunately, Palladio's three grand thermal windows that penetrated the vault of the main hall have been closed, apparently for centuries; probably the end one made it difficult to see the huge and celebrated *Marriage at Cana*, now in the Louvre, which Paolo Veronese painted for the wall below while Palladio was at work. Two monumental Corinthian font-aediculas of rose marble in the ante-room are Palladio's most imposing essays in ecclesiastical furnishing (his altars are all rather dull).

The Venetian character of the San Giorgio cloister is far removed from Palladio's other cloister design, for the monastery of the Carità in Venice,

87. Monastery of Santa Maria della Carità, unfinished court

of which only one wing is preserved in the court of the Accademia di Belle Arti [87–9]. There, Palladio explained, the attempt was not only to be Roman, but actually to recreate a grandiose Roman house which in the *Quattro Libri* he used to illustrate the Corinthian atrium. This awesome space (never built), with its columns two storeys high, is flanked by a sacristy (preserved) and chapter house that masquerade as *tablinia* [88]. Palladio knew the Roman house from Vitruvius's description rather than from ancient remains, so that his reconstruction is guesswork [cf. 38]; in fact, he made no effort to present the cloister as a *peristylium*, but used motives from the Theatre of Marcellus and the Colosseum in a context

88. Monastery of Santa Maria della Carità, plan and section

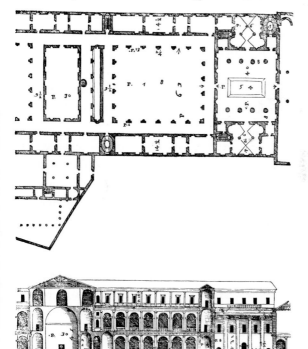

that is much closer to Bramante – except that it has a warm brick colour – than to antiquity. Two surviving pieces of the original design, the external façade of the cloister wing and an oval spiral staircase with an open well [89], are of a vital simplicity as little Renaissance as it is ancient. But in all, the design is anachronistically classical in the unclassical mid-Cinquecento; probably it seemed provincial and out-of-date to the Venetians, who were not as avid antiquarians as the Vicentines, and for the rest of his career in Venice, Palladio avoided the archaeological mode. How can the Canons have wanted, or allowed, such a showy Vitruvian revival ? Their ambitions apparently were rather worldly.

The transcendent feature of Palladio's church interiors is a light that penetrates every corner with its warmth – a light as unique and as Venetian as that created on canvas by his contemporaries Titian and Veronese. It is produced partly by the large number and size of windows, by the orientation of the plan toward the path of the sun and by the dominance of the church over surrounding buildings; but above all, it is the nature of the reflecting surfaces that endows it with a special cast of humanity, even of sensuality, and differentiates it from the austere effects of equally well-lit late Gothic interiors.

Whatever is not architecture in these churches is set apart in niches and panels; no sculpture or painted ornament invades the surfaces of walls, vaults or domes. Those surfaces, and most of the half-columns, pilasters, and entablatures, except for the parts requiring detailed carving, are stucco over brick, and must perforce be painted. Palladio could control in this way the colour and quality as well as the quantity of light. The matt stucco surfaces reflect the light candidly, and unevenly enough to reveal the human touch, as brush-strokes do in a painting. Normally, the paint is renewed every few years, restoring the church to its pristine brilliance. Stone surfaces, by contrast, are difficult to maintain, and tend to darken; in the Redentore, the details that are in stone are now somewhat

89. Monastery of Santa Maria della Carità, stairway

darker than the stucco. The white or cream stucco interior was a Venetian invention, employed in similarly uncomplicated contexts in the early Renaissance, most effectively by Mauro Coducci (Santa Maria Formosa, 1492); it may have started in churches modelled on San Marco but lacking endowments sufficient to provide walls and domes of mosaic and stone veneers. Elsewhere in Italy, frescoes covered vaults and domes, and usually were detrimental to the architectural effect (since the architect lost control of both colour and form), but in Venice this kind of monumental art had no vogue in the sixteenth and seventeenth centuries. Actually, Palladio's interiors were closer to the spirit of contemporary Venetian painting than if they had been decorated; both architecture and painting created artificial theatres for the play of a natural light.

The light does more than illumine; in the Redentore, its different quality in each of the three major spaces underlines the individuality so distinctly established in the plan; it separates the diffusedly lit nave from the amply lit tribune from the brilliantly lit monk's choir [72, 73]; but, in so doing, it really unifies, because the white blaze of the choir, against which the columns in a hemicycle are silhouetted and become immaterial, attracts one as if to a supernal goal. The spiritual implication is reinforced by a physical rise in the level of the crossing and choir, as the nave is above the ground level of the exterior [70]. Stairs are used to similar psychological effect in giving eminence to some of the villas [21, 35].

Clearly defined sequences of self-sufficient spaces in the Redentore represent Palladio's intellectual resolution of the problem of joining a domed crossing to an extended nave. Within his – or any other – classical system, it is a great advance over San Giorgio, where the crossing is, and yet is not, part of the nave. The chancel and choir are only partly integrated spaces. But San Giorgio is too exhilarating to be dismissed by classical punctilio; its openness and imperfect variety give it a vitality that is somewhat submerged in the sombre nobility of the Redentore.

The sober self-examination that produced Palladio's innovations in church planning is unrelated to the prevailing Mannerist culture or to the search for the new and stylish that characterized the attitude of many contemporaries and was enunciated by Vasari. Its ties even to the Humanist tradition are superficial, being limited to some overt references to antiquity such as the temple-front facade motive, or the niches in the choir of San Giorgio ([82]: a reconstruction of the 'frontispiece of Nero' or Temple of Jupiter on the Quirinal in Rome shown in *Quattro Libri*, IV, xii). For the most part, what Palladio took from Roman building was chosen to gain certain structural improvements and certain effects of shape, light and space that served his programme. He was equally ready to learn from Byzantine and Gothic architecture; the Imperial baths were important not so much because they were ancient as because they had some of the grandest effects one could find in the architecture of the past.

Yet Palladio was not in revolt against his time. Like Vignola in some of his later work, he was a non-Mannerist rather than an anti-Mannerist. His inventive processes were not guided by polemic, but by an earnest, even a moral impulse to find answers worthy of the challenges posed by sixteenth-century Christianity. This did not make him an architect of the Counter-Reformation, either, whatever that might be; like Venice herself, he kept his independence.

5: Principles of Palladio's Architecture

'Since architecture, like all the other arts, imitates nature, nothing (in it) can satisfy that is foreign from what is found in nature' *Quattro Libri*, I, xx

How can Palladio have derived the sophisticated purity of his designs from nature? He explains only that to be 'natural' is to be rational in structure and practical in design. Supports, for example, must be, and appear to be, adequate to the load; and pediments, since they protect openings from water, should not be broken at the top. But there was far more to this naturalism than good engineering: Palladio's Humanist training taught him that the supreme and logical Order that permeates all of God's creations should be 'imitated' in the creations of men. The imitation of nature was quite the opposite of copying what one sees around; it was a search for abstract principles. Palladio's view of architecture as natural philosophy helps to explain unique qualities in his design, especially a subtlety of proportion, composition and equilibrium, that have been praised through the centuries but seldom examined critically.

A unique feature of Palladio's sketches or the plates to his *Quattro Libri* is the uniformity of schema in plans and elevations: a triadic composition with a central block built around the axis of the entranceway, and two symmetrical flanking blocks. This is such a familiar formula of classical architecture and of Venetian architecture from its Byzantine roots, that it would not seem at all remarkable if it did not differ from the prevailing Renaissance practice in Tuscany and Rome. A characteristic central Italian building of the time, like the Palazzo Farnese in Rome, was planned without such relationships of parts. The façade had major openings at the centre, and to this extent an axis and symmetry, but otherwise it was one big rectangle perforated at regular intervals by windows. On each floor rooms of different sizes and heights were distributed according to need, and the major stairway was fitted into a corner of the court. Practices of this sort left little opportunity for an aesthetic of proportion. In the façade, only the floor heights were susceptible to proportioning (by courses and cornices), but on the death of Sangallo, the first architect of the Palazzo Farnese, his successor, Michelangelo, was able to raise the uppermost storey substantially. Palladio, by contrast, kept full control of width and depth as well as height relationships in his central block, in his lateral blocks, and in the interrelationship of all these to the whole aspect, both in elevation and in plan. The design was thus tightly knit as an organism.

The evolution of this truly three-dimensional approach to design is related to contemporary developments in mathematics. In 1573 Sylvio Belli, a friend of Palladio and fellow charter-member of the Accademia Olimpica, published a book, *On Proportions and Proportionality*, in which he set forth the well-established arithmetical principles by which Palladio worked. Belli describes proportion as if it were a cardinal virtue: 'the very source of just distribution, of beauty and of health.' Beauty is included because it is 'a correspondence of all parts arranged in their proper place'; that is, as an aspect of proportion, rather than *vice versa*, as we should describe it. Palladio applied a similar aesthetic to designs that give much more importance to proportional relationships than those of earlier Renaissance architects.

A proportion, in the system of Belli, of Palladio, and also of Barbaro's commentary on Vitruvius, is the relation of two quantities (e.g., 6 : 4), such as the height and width of a wall or the length and breadth of a room. To extend a proportional relation into three dimensions so that the wall and the floor plan could be integrated, they used what they called a 'proportionality', or 'the relationship of proportions', in which three or more terms could be linked (e.g., 9 : 6 : 4). The numbers are integrated in this example, which illustrates a 'geometric' proportion, because $\frac{9}{6} = \frac{6}{4}$. Another relevant type of proportionality was called 'harmonic' (6 : 4 : 3, or $\frac{6-4}{6} = \frac{4-3}{3}$). It was closely related to musical theory and was difficult to explain and to calculate before the invention of modern notation, so that Belli does not examine it in his book. The system has been brilliantly discussed by Rudolf Wittkower, who also explains how these 3-term formulas can be extended into series so that not only rooms and façades can be designed proportionally, but whole plans. Palladio often used harmonic proportionalities, though there is no indication in his writings that he was adept at mathematics – he could have taken his numbers from ready-made tables. Whatever their source, numbers related by proportionality are indicated in every design in the *Quattro Libri*, though in many cases structural or utilitarian needs demanded the inclusion of unrelated measurements. That numerical equivalents of the terms of *musical* harmonies could, when applied to spatial relationships in architecture, make *visual* 'harmonies', seemed to Palladio and his contemporaries to indicate a universal Design, and to validate their philosophy and their insistence on mathematics as a fundamental discipline.

The triadic system was not only suited to the use of proportionalities, but was supported by utility and by tradition. The typical Venetian house, like the traditional church, had a big central hall running from front to rear that was used as both a place of assembly and an access to other rooms. Palladio specifically affirms this tradition (*Quattro Libri*, I, xxi), and adds that the hall is to be an entranceway on the ground floor and a great *sala* on the upper floors. Elevations also have to be triadic. Loggias, Palladio says, are to be put in the front and rear of a house: if there is one, it goes in the centre (flanked by wall planes); if there are two, on either side. The same is true for staircases. The design grows from the central circulation core:

The rooms must be put on one or the other part of the entrance area or hall, and one must be aware that those to the right should correspond and be equal to those on the left so that the building is the same on one side as the other, and therefore the walls will sustain the weight of the roof equally since, if there are large rooms on one side and small ones on the other, the latter will be more able to sustain the weight by reason of the mass of the wall.

The rule is consistent with Palladio's practice, but its explanation in engineering terms is a feeble example of the author's naturalism, encouraged, perhaps, by Sylvio Belli's representation of motion or instability as being caused by 'inequality'. If it were correct, all Roman palaces would have collapsed, and some of Palladio's, too, because his rule applies only to roofing systems in which the beams or vaults are all parallel to the main axis. The roof of Palazzo Chiericati, for example, is perpendicular to the main axis, which is the short one [52, 53], and could not have followed Palladio's precept without becoming ludicrously peaked.

The Chiericati plan, however, is longer and narrower than later ones, in most of which Palladio was able to identify the structural spine with the axis, as his philosophy required. So the roofs illustrated in the *Quattro Libri* [29] are much higher than those of contemporary architects, and higher in the illustrations than in the buildings, where the principle was not observed strictly [28].

The Chiericati plan [53, 90] is typical in that the left side mirrors the right but the front does *not* mirror the rear. The exceptional cases of symmetry about two axes like the Villa Rotonda [32] allowed too little flexibility. In the Chiericati type, the building is biomorphic: the human body also is symmetrical on either side but not in depth; axial features are single, like the nose and mouth, and lateral elements paired, like the eyes and arms. Just these parallels to the body were stated by Michelangelo at the same period, and there are house plans by him of around 1518 that prophesy Palladio's. But Michelangelo's naturalism was strictly biomorphic and did not admit mathematical abstractions.

Centralized designs like the Villa Rotonda also derive from this idea, but the system is radial rather than axial, and the central dome makes the structure crablike rather than vertebrate. The dome expresses, aside from its symbolic connotations, the uniformity of the plan, the de-emphasis of axis. But even in the Rotonda, one axis dominates almost imperceptibly, being slightly wider. Palladio thought of strict uniformity as literally unnatural; this his neo-Classical admirers never understood.

The perfected Palladian style with its mathematical and structural integration of parts did not emerge at once. Early works show the concept in embryo: the central spine of Villa Godi at Lonedo [11], consisting of a stair, an atrium and a *salone*, is simply inserted into a rectangular block rather than being integrated into it by interlocking parts or by the proportions of the plan or elevation, and the low arcaded wings to the side seem to have been stuck on as an afterthought.

The design of Palazzo Chiericati [52] was inspired by two traditions: that of the medieval row house with covered street arcades, which Palladio had already revived in the Casa Civena [45], and that of a stoa-like public building alongside a square, like the Basilica, the Library in Venice ([4], 1537), or Michelangelo's Capitoline Hill (1538). Both caused a conflict between the external and public function, which required circulation along the front, and the internal private or official function, which required finding an entrance and going inside. This duality was recognized by the client, Girolamo Chiericati, who began his petition of March 1551 for a building permit:

I have been advised by expert architects and by many revered citizens to make a portico along the façade of my house on the Isola for greater convenience to me and for the convenience and ornamentation of the entire city. This opinion I have carefully considered in view of the much greater expense than would be involved without the portico; nevertheless, because of the greater convenience and the greater honour both to myself and to the public, it would be especially gratifying and rewarding to me if permission were conceded with the good graces of this magnificent city.

The public function suggests unbroken horizontal continuity; the private, stability around a central portal, hence vertical emphasis. Palladio elegantly resolved this conflict, though his site was neither a street nor a square, but an empty, shapeless area called the Isola at the edge of town not far from the river bank. He made a central, vertical emphasis by a triadic composition (in his first sketch, the central portion is topped by a pediment), and a horizontal emphasis by the unusual length of the palace in relation to its depth [53]. The extension in length produced an innovation in plan as well as in elevation: the entrance hall became a circus, taking on the form that Palladio might have imagined for an ideally urbanized Isola; it is the great hall of the Venetian palace turned ninety degrees. The triadic division is made functional as well as formal by assigning the central core from front to rear solely to circulation: hall, loggia and staircases, spiral stairs. The formula is potentially effective, though in this plan it produced a disproportion of circulation over living space.

The axis of the entrance hall crosses the principal axis and each room in turn has a cross-axis [90]. From the centre of the two lateral façade rooms, the whole depth of the building is revealed, and either a window or a fireplace marks the end of every axis. This co-ordination of a plan by cross-vistas has only one precedent in Renaissance architecture: the villa of Poggio a Caiano outside Florence, where Palladio was also anticipated in adapting the temple pediment to domestic architecture.

The plan is unified proportionally, too. In a sequence of rooms there is not only an ascending or descending order of size, but a relationship of number: one dimension of the preceding room is retained while the other changes. The smallest is 12' x 18'; its neighbour, 18' x 18', then 18' x 30'. The hall, 16' x 54', surely was meant at the start to be 18' deep, which would have made all measurements multiples of 6', but was reduced by Palladio – who could be as practical as he was abstract – because the greater width would have pushed the crown of the vault into the upper

90. Palazzo Chiericati, circulation diagram

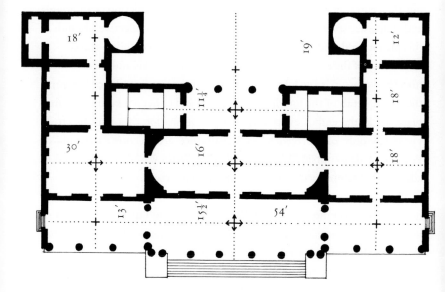

storey. The numbers are not rounded off arbitrarily, but in order to achieve particular proportions: those quoted are 2 : 3, 1 : 1, 3 : 5, 1 : 3. They correspond to musical harmonies as measured in distances on a monochord: a fifth, unison, a major sixth, and two octaves. Knowledge of this link between music and architecture came from Pythagoras and was introduced into architectural theory by Alberti just a century before the building of Palazzo Chiericati.

Palladio seems to have been especially attracted to musical proportions early in his career. The Palazzo Iseppo Porto of 1552 [56], as an example, is the only building in the *Quattro Libri* for which a number of room dimensions are indicated in three dimensions and conform to the harmonic system: the entrance atrium is 30′ square and 24′ high, with an Ionic order of 15′; the room above is 30′ x 40′ and 30′ high, and the side rooms are 20′ x 30′ x 20′. In works after this period Palladio did not so much abandon harmonics as relax in his application of them.

What differentiates Palladio's proportions from Alberti's is that they are used in integrated systems that bind plan and elevation, interior and exterior, room and room, giving a sense of the pervasiveness of the architect's control. Alberti may have dreamed of such mastery of harmony, but did not succeed in co-ordinating groups of elements in three dimensions. Like all early Renaissance architects, he designed by addition rather than by integration. Only one of his buildings – San Andrea in Mantua – has any relationship of interior to exterior, and there the one proportion in depth (of façade elevation to nave elevation) is 1 : 1 – unity rather than harmony, and unity achieved at the cost of a façade that doesn't quite cover the front of the church.

Only measured drawings can show how much the ideal proportions of the projects published in the *Quattro Libri* were carried out in building; the plates of the neo-Classical architect Bertotti Scamozzi 'correct' the buildings according to an aesthetic foreign to Palladio. The Villa Emo, as shown in two recent surveys, is built with a precision of measurement rare in the Renaissance [91]. The rooms at the four corners of the *piano nobile* and the porch were found to be the same width within a few centimetres, and the great *sala* precisely square. There are slight variations in proportion from the measurements found in the plan and elevation of the *Quattro Libri*, but the major rooms are within 10 cms. of Palladio's design, a margin of error that is encountered anyway at this scale in translating from metres to ancient Vicentine feet. The few figures Palladio gave for the elevation also correspond to the executed building. The proportion of the main portal and the windows of the *piano nobile* is precisely 2 : 1 on the exterior surface, which is the ratio of one side of the corner rooms to their height, and of the width of the ramp to its length. The *sala* is 27' square and 20' high, which is no simple harmony; the latter figure was chosen by Palladio for the height of the façade portico, and may have been projected simply for this reason onto the interior elevations.

Palladio's buildings have a hierarchy of parts: the plan and elevation not only are divided into an uneven number of vertical sections but are divided so that the central section dominates the sides and acts as the climax of the composition. Similarly, parts nearer the centre are larger and more important than those farther off. The central section is the locus, in plan, of the entranceway – usually a stair and portico in the villas and an 'atrium' in the palaces – and principal *sala* and frequently, in elevation, of a pediment supported on the columns of the portico, which raises the centre above the wings and is another way of suggesting dominance.

This core, bound to the wings by proportional relationships, is the head and torso of the body; the central axis is its spine. Only certain city palaces lack the dominant centre because they are on narrow streets that prevent them from being seen properly from a standpoint directly opposite; these adopt the central Italian tradition of continuous horizontals that take up the axis of the street. But wherever there was enough space to

91. Villa Emo, plan, compared to Palladio's project

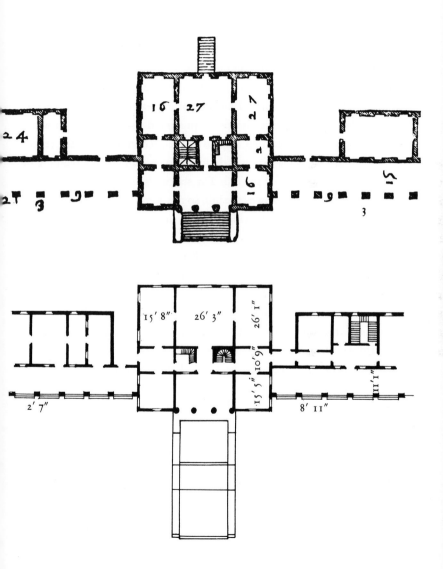

allow a view of the façade from some distance, the dominant centre appears, as in palaces planned for squares or broad streets. In the villas, the hierarchy not only affects the massing of the house itself, but establishes a dominance of house over porticoes and barns, and of barns over outlying walls (at Fratta Polesine [29], the physical hierarchy is reinforced by a hierarchy of vocabulary : the simpler Tuscan order is used for the wings, and the more elegant Ionic for the central portico). And the design was not limited to the structures. Evidence of a greater framework, encompassing the surrounding landscape, is preserved in some villas in which both topography and planting emphasize the predominance of the central building. Villa Rotonda [33] was designed to be seen not as a building on a hill but as the summit of the hill. The stairways assume the slope of the terrain and, as the villa crowns the hill, so the dome, rising from the gentle slope of the roof, crowns the villa. The site urged a central plan with arms radiating from the core.

Because of its radiating system, the Rotonda looks equally good from all viewpoints in a 360° arc, but this is not true of other free-standing villas in which one or two façades dominate, as at Malcontenta. There, a view from an angle reveals side façades that are not especially well proportioned or well co-ordinated with those of the front and rear, because the plan is rectangular, and symmetrical about one axis only. The project in the *Quattro Libri* would have masked the conflict by putting large courts on either side of the villa with high walls hiding all but the upper parts of the side elevations, but they were not built. In most of the villas, loggia-wings screen the inevitable awkwardness of the side facades. Every 'hieratic' exterior should be seen from a more-or-less central position before it. This makes Palladio's work the antithesis of Michelangelo's, which demands motion through and around. Rigour of proportions put restrictions on the observer's action, though not severely confining ones. If some of Palladio's designs lack scenographic, perspective qualities, it is because the nature of his system demanded that these be suppressed in favour of the geometry of the front and rear.

Palladio attributed his sort of hierarchy of elements to the ancients. Whenever he reproduced the plan of a complex Greek or Roman building or building-group, it appeared to have a dominant centre and an equal number of subordinate parts on either side. The obviously irregular ancient sites that he studied, such as Hadrian's Villa in Tivoli, never found their way into a publication or even a clean finished drawing.

Did Palladio get the idea of hieratic design from observing Roman structures or did he impose his own rationalism on what he saw in the ruins and read in Vitruvius? Judging by his reconstructions of ancient villas and houses [38], he imagined a characteristically Renaissance order of a kind that did not interest the ancient Romans. Excavations have shown that they were nearly always casual in domestic planning and that symmetry and a hierarchy of parts was exceptional. But public building, particularly in Imperial times, sometimes contained features of the Palladian system beyond an obvious predilection for central axes and cross-axes as fulcra for symmetrical composition.

The Imperial baths came closest to Palladio's ideal. Actually, they were the only class of ancient structure that could stimulate solutions to many of his planning problems, which was one reason why he prepared for publication a graphic survey of all the baths in Rome (published in part from his drawings, but only in 1730).

While the baths of the Republic and early Empire had been casual and asymmetrical in plan, the huge Imperial establishments from the time of Titus and Trajan on, which were the most accessible to the Renaissance antiquarian, began to be built around a grandiose sequence of axial spaces progressing from the great pool to the Frigidarium, Tepidarium and Calidarium. These aulae had probably taken over the central core of the building not because the major functions were thought to deserve it (the entrance, for example, had to be off-centre, because the undressing rooms were not included in the core), but because they came to be accommodated in immense vaulted spaces the structural imperatives of which could be met best by a central position. Size rather than significance determined the massing. None of the great halls had priority and the exteriors did not even differentiate the core from the wings.

When Palladio studied the remains of the poorly preserved or partly buried baths such as those of Agrippa, he recorded faithfully what he found, in sketches made on the site which in this case gave no promise of yielding a symmetrical scheme. But he returned to his studio to 'reconstruct' a strictly Palladian plan in which even the motives that survived in the ruins were lost [93]. In the case of better preserved monuments like the Baths of Caracalla, which is the Roman building closest to Palladio in composition, the reconstructions are accurate. The sections, however, are chosen in such a way that, without actually misinforming, they conspire to make the design look more Palladian than it really is. All the major spaces in [92] are subservient to a commanding dome over the Calidarium which now is thought to have been no higher than the vaults of the Frigidarium (actually the main room), and which anyway would have been invisible from three of the four sides of the Baths. But the drawing accurately shows how the Baths, like most Palladian buildings, are symmetrical about only the short axis; the section in depth at the bottom is asymmetrical.

Palladio's version of the baths has been so appealing and so useful to later generations that it has escaped criticism. Archaeologists, knowing that the ruins were better preserved in Palladio's time, have been influenced subtly by his taste for order as well as by his precious information; their reconstructions favour symmetry and hierarchy, too. But surely Palladio was more of a rationalist than the Romans.

In the baths and in comparable Roman structures, units of space are simply assembled in an orderly fashion. The Romans liked interesting and

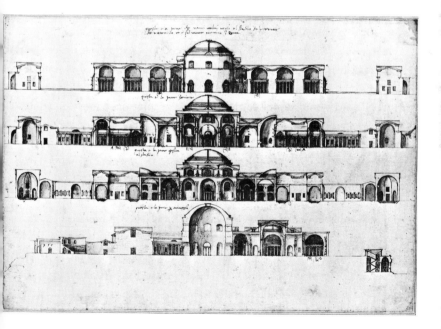

varied interior spatial volumes and sequences of volumes, and did not think much about exteriors. They did not use Palladio's mathematical methods of integrating a plan, but they did suggest to him visual methods. From the centre of major spaces in the baths there are often vistas of further areas along a major axis, forward and back, and along a cross-axis, to the right and left [93]. In this way, the entrance of Palazzo Chiericati [90] is a descendant of the Frigidarium in the Baths of Caracalla.

The casual sketches that Palladio made in preparing the book on baths are especially Roman in spirit [93]. They analyse an agglomeration of spaces around a core that differs radically from the architect's own method of geometric sub-division. It is the experience of being *in* the building that Palladio records here, rather than his assumptions about the designer's method of composition. This experience entered into his church design, particularly at the Redentore [71], where a sequence of visually integrated yet clearly distinguished vaulted spaces recalls the relationships in [93]. For example, the nave does not merge into the crossing; instead, their separateness is emphasized, and the nave space is experienced as an independent box, like the Frigidarium of the Baths of Caracalla or of Diocletian.

If Palladio's innovations in the planning of interior space were stimulated by the baths, his novel ideas of massing – the grouping of distinct building elements – were indebted to one of the most impressive religious complexes of the ancient world, the Temple of Fortuna Primigenia at Praeneste [94]. This vast Hellenistic grouping of structures on which modern Palestrina is founded covered a mountain-side. Ramps, terraces, and halls rose for hundreds of feet up the slope of a mountain to give a monumental foundation for a crowning precinct. Palladio drew it often; first in an admirably exact survey, and later in various fantastic reconstructions. Recent excavations – aided, paradoxically, by bombings in the last war – suggest that Palladio interpreted the temple as he had the baths, in emphasizing, without actual misrepresentation, a focus at the core and a

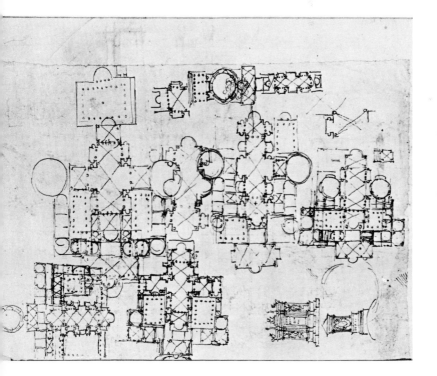

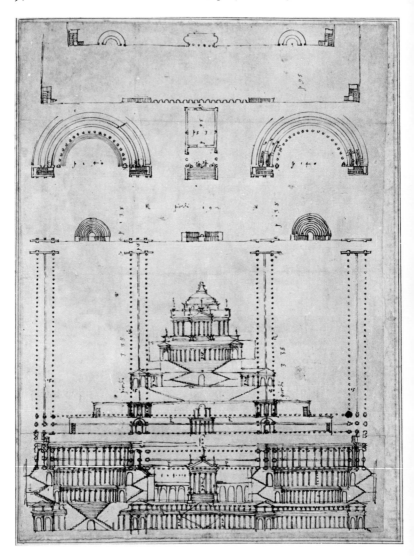

climax at the summit, where he put a great round temple as a crowning feature. Foundations for a somewhat smaller temple exist at this point, but the Italian excavators believe that much of it was meant to be hidden behind the semi-circular loggia. A distinguished German archaeologist, however, prefers the Palladian interpretation on aesthetic and symbolic grounds, which recalls the old Italian adage *'se non è vero, è ben trovato'*.

In any case, Palladio's inventiveness is more to the point than his accuracy. He must have been drawn to Praeneste because in designing hillside villas with diverse functions he would have sought useful precedents, and there were none in the Middle Ages or Renaissance. As with the baths, when he 'discovered' the right monument, he saw it as an answer to his own problems as well as an archaeological site to be reconstructed. Praeneste taught ways of visually reforming a hill-side and means of functional and structural access to a summit which emerge in the design for Villa Trissino in Meledo [35], the purest example of the hieratic principle. It was to become one of Palladio's most influential works, affecting Le Vau's Collège des Quatre Nations in Paris, Vanbrugh's Blenheim Castle, and perhaps even Bernini's Piazza di San Pietro. Among other Palladio designs derived from the Fortuna temple are the Hellenic post-and-lintel loggias [29] which in the Renaissance were rarely found elsewhere on ancient buildings.

In the early years of the century Bramante also had been stimulated by Praeneste, when he was changing the hill-side of the Vatican into the Cortile del Belvedere. He used the ramps, the terraces, the hemicycle at the summit, but, as he was looking for effects of mass, he was less interested than Palladio in the light and airy colonnades. Every great architect finds his own antiquity.

In one case, Palladio's antiquity is that of the Humanist scholars – learned, archaeological, conscious of the past rather than modern. This was the design of a theatre and meeting halls commissioned by his fellow members of the Accademia Olimpica in Vicenza. The Teatro Olimpico [95, 96] is all of wood, like the Renaissance theatres before it, which have disappeared together with a unique stone one built by Falconetto in Loreo for Alvise Cornaro in 1528. It is preserved partly by sheer luck and partly by being the only Renaissance theatre built for and maintained by an institution that has lasted for over four hundred years.

Renaissance theatre, successor to the medieval miracle plays and sacred pageants, emerged during the fifteenth century in two forms: popular, often dialect, plays that usually were comedies, and Humanist drama of the intelligentsia and *signori*, mostly tragedy, in imitation of the Greek theatre. It was the Humanist strain that excited interest in an architectural setting: first for the actors, and later for the audience, too, toward the end of the fifteenth century. Some of the earliest stage designs come from the Milanese circle of Bramante, in the 1490s. Naturally, in a Humanist culture, the effort to restore ancient drama was accompanied by an effort to re-create ancient stage design, and for this, as for most other rebirths, Vitruvius was the chief written source. His text, always obscure, is denser than usual in the passages on the theatre, but its description of illusionistic perspective scenery suited the early Renaissance passion for perspective, and led to a formula, developed by Peruzzi and illustrated by Serlio, of stage platforms backed by city streets (or landscapes for pastoral plays) made by tricks of foreshortening to look as real as possible. The early designers were satisfied to concentrate on scenery and the stage, but Palladio, whose attitude was more archaeological, was bent on applying his knowlege of the remains of ancient theatres to a revival of the whole structure.

The first sign of his involvement with theatrical architecture is his reconstruction of Vitruvius's theatre for Daniele Barbaro's 1556 edition, on the basis of his study of the surviving remains at Verona, Rome, Pola and particularly at the 'Berga' theatre in Vicenza itself (now wholly hidden). The illustrations, which Barbaro credits to Palladio, might be at the same time initial studies for the Teatro Olimpico and reconstructions of the Berga ruins. The street perspectives shown in the archways of the elevation woodcut are not like those of the Olimpico, but, as the plan shows, are painted on flats inserted in the archways. Following Vitruvius's prescription, the flats have three faces and can be rotated to change the scene. Later archaeologists proved that Palladio misread the text: the scenery should not be in the proscenium openings, or behind them, as in the Teatro Olimpico, but alongside. Still, Palladio's amalgam of his conflicting sources was as scientific as was possible at that moment.

In the years following the Vitruvius edition, Palladio had opportunities to try out his ideas. In the late 1550s the Academy began to sponsor a series of elaborate stage performances. Palladio did not design the first of them, but in 1561 he was asked to build a theatre in the great hall of the Basilica for the performance of *L'amor costante* by Piccolomini. In the following year, Trissino's tragedy *Sofonisba* was performed on a still larger stage, capable of accommodating eighty actors, with both urban and rustic perspectives, now in three dimensions. Both structures, as portrayed in frescoes of the 1590s, are of the Olimpico type, though the prosceniums differ in design; except that they were unroofed, they can not have been cheaper to build. Nothing is preserved of another theatre of 1564–5 made for the Compagnia della Calza degli Accesi in the cloister of the Carità Monastery in Venice, which Palladio was still building. All we know of it is Vasari's statement that it was like the Colosseum and that Federico Zuccari designed twelve *storie* for it, probably to put in the bays of the proscenium. The comparison with the Colosseum suggests a four-tiered exterior façade, which is lacking at the Teatro Olimpico because its exteriors were left to chance and hidden by neighbouring buildings.

In 1579, the Academy voted to build a permanent theatre with contributions from its membership. The land was ceded by the Commune in February, 1580, and work started immediately, following a model already prepared by Palladio. An original drawing survives showing alternative proposals for the proscenium and a section of the *cavea* [95]. The right side is close to the executed design, though a number of changes were made, some of them probably by Palladio since much of the construction was done by the time of his death in August 1580. The perspectives were not started in the first campaign, for lack of land acquired later. Scamozzi designed and built them in 1584–5, and probably raised the heights of the side doors to favour the perspectives [96]. The allegorical figures proposed in Palladio's drawing were transformed by vote of the academicians in the spring of 1580 into heroic likenesses of themselves; just at the moment when Vicenza's noblemen had to abandon all hope of ever being heroes in fact.

Palladio could not have watched the building closely in his last months, and his executors made a number of unfortunate decisions. The ceiling over the stage, in Palazzo Ducale style, is irrelevant, and other parts, such as the transition from the stage to the *cavea*, seem to have been left to chance. But the theatre is still impressive as a fantasy that enfolds the visitor in a past world. More than this, it has had a power to preserve the Renaissance itself: every year it attracts people of every nation to its classically bruising seats to attend performances of classic drama. Without the Teatro Olimpico, Sophocles and Racine would not be played in modern Vicenza or, if they were, the world would not come to watch.

Palladio's archaeological theatre was a poorly adapted mutant in the evolution of its species; the type did not survive in competition with contemporary innovations in Florence where theatres were being built with regular rectangular halls, a proscenium arch, a curtain at the front of the stage, and unencumbered space behind for scenery. After 1580, the Humanist spirit that made the Olimpic Academy and theatre possible was less productive and influential than the courtly spirit that promoted the seventeenth-century illusionist stage, the masque and the opera. Palladio

95. Proscenium of the Teatro Olimpico

himself, to judge from his other late works, had lost interest in the kind of literal revival that his theatre represents. He reached back, in deference to his fellow academicians, to a moment in his own development that he had passed.

So the theatre does not typify Palladio's relation to antiquity; for the most part he sought in Roman architecture ways of organizing and of integrating complexes of spaces and masses, especially in patterns grouped about a central axis composed of major spaces. But these lessons were simply a stimulus for the formulation of principles *not* manifest in ancient design, which may be defined as follows:

1. Hierarchy, or the systematic build-up from dependent parts to a focal core.
2. The integration by proportionality, in three dimensions, of part to part and part to whole.
3. The co-ordination of exterior and interior design by representing the interior organization on the façades and by consistency in the proportional system.

Is Palladio's architecture 'classical'? If the term means 'in the spirit of ancient Greece and Rome', it fits only certain works like the Teatro Olimpico, and even these, loosely. Palladio loved the ruins but, like most lovers, he saw only what, and how, he wanted. He could be irrational, using elements of ancient architecture pictorially rather than tectonically. Admiring the effect of temple porticoes, he would put them on villas, or cut them up and put pieces of them on churches. On his late Vicentine façades, he used the orders like brush-strokes. Or he could be vigorously philosophical, in imposing on the design process a method that in diluted form affected Western architecture for four hundred years, and seems especially potent today. He was not classical, then, in the sense of being a

reviver of antiquity; or anyway he was less so than Bramante, Sangallo, or Jacopo Sansovino, and as little, perhaps, as Michelangelo.

Nor was Palladio classical like Raphael or Andrea Sansovino, who accepted a tradition in Western art in which logic and organization – *disegno* in the critical vocabulary of the time – take precedence over the senses. If he is seen as a planner or a maker of harmonies – the Palladio of the *Quattro Libri* – then he does indeed seem to be of that tradition. But another Palladio, unknown to many of the classicists who revered the book but never visited the Veneto, is the magician of light and colour, the architectural counterpart of Veronese. The cerebral theoretician evaporates from the consciousness of the visitor who steps through the door of San Giorgio Maggiore to be greeted by an engagingly illogical and complex surrounding transformed by a warm and varied light into an environment in its own way as supernatural as that of a Gothic cathedral dissolved in the hues of its stained glass. Palladio was as sensual, as skilled in visual alchemy as any Venetian painter of his time. He loved modulating light, and introduced unheard-of colours and textures into architecture or used the familiar ones in unheard-of combinations. It is the fusion of the intellectual and the sensuous in Palladio that has made him the favourite of so many generations and so many different types of westerners, in a way that the true classicists like Raphael and the true sensualists like Veronese have not been.

Since the Romantic period we have polarized the intellect and the senses until one is believed to exclude the other. Classicists are only rational and romantics are only sensual or emotional. But the best Palladian critics were those early enough to accept the complexity of his work, and outstanding among these was the most passionate, the most 'classical' Venetian of the seventeenth century, Baldassare Longhena.

Venice was enveloped for centuries in the spell cast by Palladio's architecture. The rest of Europe succumbed in the eighteenth century, in a purist reaction against the excesses and preciosity of late Baroque and Rococo architecture. The reformers of the Age of Enlightenment understood only the rationalist Palladio of the *Quattro Libri* and the drawings- which had passed fortuitously into England, the most enthusiastic and influential of Palladian nations. They hardly knew him at first hand. The villas, which were his most imitated works, were hard to get to, and anyway the Palladians were trying to eradicate the very qualities that differentiated the real works from the graphic records of them. The only understanding and sympathetic judge of that age was one in whom supreme powers of intellect and of the senses were combined : Goethe.

The neo-Classicists and their nineteenth-century followers looked on Palladio as the discoverer of some divine, or at least eternal, law in architecture. Simplified versions of his system of proportional relationships and of organizing a plan and elevation were represented as most attuned to human physical and psychological make-up in their appeal to permanently valid laws of harmony and in their reference to the structure of the human body. But the music and art of the twentieth century and our enlarged knowledge of distant and primitive cultures have challenged any claim to natural pre-eminence of certain consonances or organizations of form. Palladio's harmony was not more than an ingenious product of Humanism which his great sensitivity equipped him to use with unparalleled effectiveness. And, because it seemed right to so many later generations, it found what appears to be a permanent place in the making of architecture.

Bibliographical Notes

GENERAL WORKS

The basic studies on Palladio were nearly all published in the century 1750–1850 and since 1930. Of the first group the most valuable are Ottavio Bertotti Scamozzi's *Le fabbriche e i disegni di A. P.*, Vicenza, 1776 and 1786, which contains measured drawings and reconstructions of Palladio's building, often adjusted to neo-classic taste, and a historical and critical commentary to the plates. A similar and very rare predecessor by F. Muttoni (pseud. N. N.), *L'architettura di A. P.*, 9 vols., Venice, 1740–48, is less accurate. Tommaso Temanza, *Vita di A. P.*, Venice, 1762, the basis of later biographies, is useful now mostly as a document of its times. The very brief notices in Giorgio Vasari's *Vite dei pittori scultori e architetti...* (1568), ed. G. Milanesi, Florence, 1906, VII, pp. 527–31 (Life of Jacopo Sansovino), and in the Life by Paolo Gualdo of *c.*1617 (ed. G. G. Zorzi, *Saggi e Memorie*, II, 1959, pp. 93–104) are important as the sources closest to Palladio. The basis of modern scholarship is the thorough, extensively documented life by A. Magrini (*Memorie intorno la vita e le opere di A. P.*, 2 vols. in I, Padua, 1845), which still is indispensable. The major modern monographs are those of Roberto Pane, *A. P.* (2nd ed., Turin, 1961), of the late G. G. Zorzi (whose four large volumes, the fruit of a long career of valuable documentary-archival research, are devoted to the drawings, the palaces/public buildings, churches/bridges and villas/theatres are cited under the appropriate headings below), and of Lionello Puppi, *A. P.*, Boston, 1975 (Italian ed., Milan, 1973), the most penetrating of the three, which encorporates the results of the intensive scholarship of the past decade. Nicola Ivanoff's *Palladio*, Milan, 1967, is a fine summary similar to the present book in scope. The catalogues of the Palladio exhibitions in Vicenza (1973) and London (by Howard Burns, 1975) provide excellent critical and documentary texts.

The foundations of modern Palladio criticism are the essays of Rudolf Wittkower ('Principles of P.'s Architecture', and 'The Problem of Harmonic Proportion in Architecture', *Architectural Principles in the Age of Humanism*, Parts III and IV, London, 1949, 3rd ed., 1962) and G. C. Argan ('A. P. e la critica neo-classica', *L'Arte*, I, 1930, pp. 327–46; 'L'importanza di Sanmicheli nella formazione del P.', *Atti del 18° congresso internazionale di storia dell'arte*, Venice, 1950, pp. 387–9). See also F. Barbieri, 'P. e il manierismo', *Bollettino del Centro internazionale di storia dell'archi-*

tettura (hereafter, *BCIS A*), VI, 1964, pp. 49-63; idem, 'Il primo P.', *BCIS A*, IX, 1967, pp. 37-48; R. Cevese, 'Proposta per una nuova lettura critica dell'arte palladiana', *Essays in the History of Architecture Presented to Rudolf Wittkower*, London, 1967, pp. 122-7; R. Wittkower, *P. and Palladianism*, New York, 1974.

CHAPTER I

For biographical addenda since Magrini: G. G. Zorzi, 'La vera origine e la giovinezza di A. P.', *Archivio Veneto-Tridentino*, II, 1922, pp. 120-50, expanded in *Arte Veneta*, III, 1949, pp. 140-52; *Disegni delle antichità di A. P.*, Venice, 1959, Introduction, and *Le opere pubbliche e i palazzi privati di A. P.*, Venice, 1965, Appendix; A. Dalla Pozza, *Palladio,* Vicenza, 1943, ch. I (containing a proposal, since withdrawn, that Palladio was Vicentine rather than Paduan by birth); R. Gallo, 'A. P. e Venezia', *Rivista di Venezia*, n.s. I, 1955, pp. 23-47.

Palladio's cultural formation is discussed by A. Dalla Pozza, *Palladio*, ch. II; R. Wittkower, *Architectural Principles*, Part III; G. Fiocco, 'Incunabuli di A. P.', *Saggi in onore di V. Fasolo (Quaderni Ist. stor. dell'architettura*, ser. VI-VIII), Rome, 1961, pp. 169-76; 'Le lezioni di Alvise Cornaro', *BCIS A*, V, 1963, pp. 33-43; G. Piovene, 'Trissino e P. nell'umanesimo vicentino', ibid., pp. 13-23; G. Forssman, *Palladios Lehrgebäude*, Stockholm, 1965, Part III.

On specific relationships: G. C. Argan, 'Sebastiano Serlio', *L'Arte*, XXXV, 1932, pp. 183-99; G. Fiocco, 'A. Cornaro e i suoi trattati sull'architettura', *Accad. naz. dei Lincei, Atti, ser. 8, Memorie*, IV, 1952, pp. 195-222; R. Pallucchini, 'Giulio Romano e P.', *BCIS A*, I, 1959, pp. 38-44. Essays in vol. VIII of *BCIS A*, 1966, and in vol. XV, 1973, treat Palladio's debt to Raphael, Bramante, the Sangallos, Falconetto, Giulio Romano, Sansovino, Sanmicheli, Serlio and Daniele Barbaro, and his relationship to Bernini and Vignola.

On Palladio's drawings and studies of the antique: Zorzi, *I disegni delle antichità di A. P.*, Venice, 1959, *passim*, with some questionable identifications and attributions, particularly of a group of drawings to Falconetto; see the more accurate catalogue by H. Spielmann, *A.P. und die Antike*, Munich-Berlin, 1966; W. Lotz in *BCIS A*, IV, 1962, pp. 61-8, and H. Burns in the London *Catalogue* and in *BCIS A*, XV, 1973, pp. 169-91. John Harris has reported on the discovery of new drawings in Oxford in 'Three Unrecorded P. Designs', *Burlington Magazine*, CXII, 1971, pp. 34-7.

CHAPTER 2

The basis of villa studies, partly superseded by subsequent scholarship, is Fritz Burger, *Die Villen des A. P.*, Leipzig, 1909; Wittkower, in *Architectural Principles*, Part III, analyses the style; J. S. Ackerman, *P.'s Villas*, New York, 1967, a short lecture-essay surveying earlier modern research, is largely superseded by later studies; G. G. Zorzi's large monograph, *Le ville e i teatri di A. P.*, Vicenza, 1968, includes the material from his basic earlier publications on the villa drawings (in the journal *Palladio*, n.s. IV, 1954, pp. 59-76) and on sources for attribution (*Arte Veneta*, VI, 1952, pp. 135-9 and IX, 1955, pp. 95-122). A. Dalla Pozza's archival work corrected substantial errors in the dating of several buildings ('Palladiana', *Odeo olimpico*, IV, Vicenza, 1963-4, pp. 99-131, and V, 1964-5, pp. 203-16). Valuable recent studies have been F. Barbieri, 'P. in villa negli anni quaranta', *Arte Veneta*, XXIV, 1970, pp. 68-80, and L. Puppi, 'Dubbi e certezze per P. costruttore in villa', *Arte Veneta*, XXVIII, 1974, 93-105.

On the Venetian villas in general, see the catalogue, *Le ville venete*, Treviso, 1954 by G. Mazzotti and others; Mazzotti's richly illustrated *Palladian and Other Venetian Villas*, London, 1958; R. Cevese, *Ville della provincia di Vicenza*, Milan, 1971; G. F. Viviani, ed., *La villa nel Veronese*, Verona, 1975. Critical comment: Georgina Masson, 'Palladian Villas as Rural Centres', *Architectural Review*, 118, 1955, pp. 17-20; J. S. Ackerman, 'Sources of the Renaissance Villa', *Acts of the Twentieth International Congress of the History of Art*, Princeton, 1963, pp. 6-18; Michelangelo Muraro, *Civiltà delle ville venete*, Venice (privately duplicated), 1964; K. W. Forster, 'Back to the Farm . . .', *Architectura*, 1974, pp. 1-12.

Research on Venetian villas of the period preceding Palladio shows Palladio to have been more dependent on his immediate forerunners than I indicated in the first edition. See B. Rupprecht, 'Ville venete del '400 e del primo '500: forme e sviluppo', *BCISA*, VI, 1964, pp. 239-50; M. Rosci, 'Forme e funzioni delle ville venete pre-palladiane', *L'Arte*, n.s. I, 1968, pp. 25-54; Heydenreich, 'La villa: genesi e sviluppi fino al P.', *BCISA*, XI, 1969, pp. 11-21 (and numerous other villa essays in that volume); W. Prinz, *Anfänge des oberitalienische Villenbaues*, Darmstadt, 1973, and M. Kubelik, *Zur typologischen Entwicklung des Quattrocentovilla in Veneto*, Aachen, 1975.

For the economic history of Venice and its territory in the later sixteenth century I have used R. Cessi, 'Alvise Cornaro e la bonifica veneziana del sec. XVI', *Accad. dei Lincei, cl. scienze morali etc.*, 6 ser., XIII, 1936, pp. 301-23; D. Beltrami, *Saggio di storia dell'agricoltura nella Reppublica di Venezia durante l'eta moderna*, Venice-Rome,

1955; G. Luzzatto, 'La decadenza di Venezia dopo le scoperte geografiche', *Archivio Veneto*, ser. 5, LIV-LV, 1954, pp. 162ff. (good bibliography), and *Storia economica di Venezia dal XI al XVI secolo*, Venice, 1961; A. Stella, 'La crisi economica veneziana della 2ª metà del sec. XVI', *Archivio Veneto*, ser. 5, LVIII-LIX, 1956, pp. 17–69; F. Braudel, 'La vita economica di Venezia nel sec. XVI', *La civiltà veneziana del rinascimento*, Florence, 1958, pp. 81–102; S. J. Woolf, 'Venice and the Terra-firma . . .', 1962, reprinted in B. Pullan, ed., *Crisis and Change in the Venetian Economy in the Sixteenth and Seventeenth Centuries*, London, 1968; A. Ventura, *Nobiltà e popolo nella società veneta del '400 e '500*, Bari, 1964; B. Pullan, *Rich and Poor in Renaissance Venice*, Oxford, 1971.

On single villas: W. Lotz, 'La Rotonda, edificio civile con cupola', *BCISA*, IV, 1962, pp. 69–73; G. Mazzariol, *P. a Maser*, Venice, 1965; C. A. Isermeyer, 'Die Villa Rotonda von P.', *Zeitschrift für Kunstgeschichte*, 1967, pp. 207–21 (redating the famous villa from *c*.1550-53 to 1566-70); C. Semenzato, *La Rotonda di A.P.*, Vicenza, 1968 (*Corpus Palladianum*, I, the first of a series of monographs published by the CISA): L. Bordignon Favero, *La Villa Emo di Fanzolo* (*Corpus Palladianum*, V), Vicenza, 1970 (English ed., 1972); L. Puppi, *La Villa Badoer di Fratta Polesine* (*Corpus Palladianum*, VII), Vicenza, 1972. Douglas Lewis has published new documents on several villas in *BCISA*, XIV, 1972, pp. 381–93; XV, 1973, pp. 369–79.

CHAPTER 3

Modern study of the palaces began with the able book of H. Pée, *Die Palastbauten des A. P.*, Würzburg, 1941. G. G. Zorzi, *Le opere pubbliche e i palazzi privati di A. P.*, Venice, 1965, contains much new documentary material and incorporates the author's many articles on the subject (see the thorough review by R. Cevese in *BCISA*, VI, 1964, pp. 334–59). The Vicentine buildings are covered by the excellent *Guida di Vicenza* by F. Barbieri, R. Cevese and L. Magagnato, Vicenza, 2nd ed., 1956, and by Dalla Pozza, *Palladio*, chs. III-V. My publication of a large and detailed view of Vicenza with valuable data on P.'s palaces ('P.'s Vicenza: a Bird's-eye Plan of *c*.1571', *Studies in Renaissance and Baroque Art Presented to Anthony Blunt*, London, 1967, pp. 53–61) led to a more thorough study, and the publication of a facsimile, by F. Barbieri, *La pianta prospettica di Vicenza del 1580*, Vicenza, 1973.

The social and economic history of sixteenth-century Vicenza has not been studied much, but G. Mantese gives an extensive introduction to many phases of life in the later volumes of his *Memorie storiche della chiesa vicentina*, Vicenza, 1964; 1974. A useful older work is F. Formenton, *Memorie storiche della città di Vicenza*, Vicenza, 1867. On single buildings: R. Cevese, *I palazzi dei Thiene*, Vicenza, 1952; F. Barbieri, *Il museo civico di Vicenza*, I, Venice, 1962, and idem, *La basilica palladiana* (*Corpus Palladianum*, II), Vicenza, 1968 (English ed., 1971); L. Magagnato, *Il palazzo Thiene*, Vicenza, 1966; A. Venditti, *La loggia del Capitaniato* (*Corpus Palladianum*, IV), Vicenza, 1969 (English ed., 1971); B. Rupprecht, 'P.'s Projekt für den Palazzo Iseppo Porto in Vicenza', *Mitt. des Kunsthistorisch Institutes in Florenz*, XV, 1971, pp. 289-314; E. Forssman, *Il Palazzo da Porto Festa* (*Corpus Palladianum*, VIII), Vicenza, 1973.

CHAPTER 4

The ecclesiastical architecture is intensively studied in two volumes that appeared after the publication of my first edition: G. G. Zorzi, *Le chiese e i ponti di A. P.*, Vicenza, 1966, and W. Timofiewitsch, *Die sakrale Architektur Palladios*, Munich, 1968. Wittkower's critical analyses are basic: *Architectural Principles*, Part III, and 'Le chiese di A. P. e l'architettura veneta', *Barocco europeo e barocco veneziano*, Florence, 1962, pp. 77-87; his theory of 'interlocking temple-fronts' is contested by H. Lund, 'The façade of S. Giorgio Maggiore', *Architectural Review*, 133, 1963, pp. 283ff. Christian Isermeyer's paper 'Le chiese del P. in rapporto al culto' (*BCISA*, X, 1968, pp. 42-58) is a penetrating study of issues insufficiently considered in earlier literature. W. Timofiewitsch has published several important monographic studies in *Arte Veneta*, XIII-XIV, 1959-60, pp. 79-87 (projects for San Nicola di Tolentino); ibid., XVI, 1962, pp. 160-63, and *BCISA*, V, 1963, pp. 330-37 (San Giorgio Maggiore); *Arte Veneta*, XVI, 1962, pp. 82-97 (façade projects for San Petronio in Bologna; see also a further project in J. S. Ackerman, *Essays in the History of Architecture Presented to Rudolf Wittkower*, London, 1967, pp. 110-15). Timofiewitsch's *La chiesa del Redentore* (*Corpus Palladianum*, III), Vicenza, 1968 (English ed., 1971) is valuable but does not deal adequately with the problems of form posed by Sinding-Larsen in the article quoted below.

P.'s first religious work in Venice is treated in E. Bassi, *Il convento della Carità* (*Corpus Palladianum*, VI), Vicenza, 1971 (English ed., 1974).

For the history of San Giorgio, G. Damerini, *L'isola e il cenobio di San Giorgio Maggiore*, Venice, 1956, and of the Redentore, P. Davide Portogruaro, 'Il tempio e il convento del Redentore', *Rivista di Venezia*, 1930, pp. 141-224; S. Sinding-Larsen, 'P.'s Redentore, a Compromise in Composition', *The Art Bulletin*, XLVII, 1965, pp. 419-37.

CHAPTER 5

The best analyses of Palladian principles are cited above: Argan's articles of 1930 and 1950, Wittkower's *Architectural Principles,* Parts III and especially IV, and Forssman's *P.'s Lehrgebäude.* The history of Palladio criticism is reviewed by Pane in *Palladio,* ch. I.

The Teatro Olimpico has been excellently analysed by L. Magagnato, 'The Genesis of the T. O.', *Journal of the Warburg and Courtauld Institutes,* XIV, 1951, pp. 209-20, and *Il teatro italiano del Cinquecento,* Venice, 1954; and by L. Puppi, *Il Teatro Olimpico,* Vicenza, 1963; G. G. Zorzi, 'Le prospettive del T. O. di Vicenza', *Arte Lombarda,* X, 2, 1965, pp. 70-97; idem, *Le ville e i teatri di A. P.,* pp. 282-327; cf. L. Puppi, in *Arte Lombarda,* XI, 1966, pp. 26-32. Further theatre studies will appear in the forthcoming vol. XVI of the *BCISA.*

Bibliographical surveys of Palladio's work have appeared in *Zeitschr. für Kunstgeschichte,* XXIII, 1960, pp. 174-81 (Timofiewitsch); *BCISA,* III, 1961, pp. 163-71 (Ferrari); *BCISA,* VII, 1965, pp. 363-91 (Ferrari); *L'Arte,* 10, 1970, pp. 114-24 (Rosci); *L'Information d'histoire de l'art,* 11, 1971, pp. 55-72 (Puppi). Puppi's 1975 monograph includes a full bibliography.

Index

Veronese, Paolo, 39-40, 48, 124, 153, 156
Vesalius, Andrea, 24
Vicenza: Accademia dei Costanti, 32, 84;
    Accademia Olimpica, 21, 31, 32, 84,
    161, 180; architecture, general, 25, 81,
    93, 94; Basilica, 14, 24, 87-92, 94, 101,
    122, 164, 179 (theatre); Berga Theatre,
    178-9; Casa Civena, 14, 30, 40, 93,
    101-3, 164; Casa Cogollo, 85; Cathe-
    dral, 15; history, 31, 32, 83-4, 87, 122;
    Isola, 101, 164-5; Loggia del Capi-
    taniato, 14, 84, 112, 117-22, 124;
    Palazzo Barbarano, 14, 104, 112-17,
    124; Palazzo Capra, project, 101;
    Palazzo Chiericati, 14, 31, 101-3, 123,
    163, 164, 167, 174; Palazzo Garza-
    dore, project, 101; Palazzo Iseppo
    Porto, 14, 103-4, 112, 117, 124, 167;
    Palazzo Porto-Barbarano, *see* Palazzo
    Barbarano; Palazzo Porto-Breganze,
    112, 117; Palazzo Schio-Angaran, 14;
    Palazzo Thiene, 14, 30, 31, 94-8, 104,
    123; Palazzo Trissino, project, 101;
    Palazzo Valmarana, 14, 31, 104, 106-
    17, 124; Piazza dei Signori, 118; Sta
    Corona, 15; Teatro Olimpico, 14, 32,
    112, 178-82; Theatre of Serlio, 24;
    Villa Cricoli, 20, 21, 43; Villa Ro-
    tonda, 14, 31, 61, 68, 80, 163, 164, 170

Wittkower, Rudolf, 20, 162

Zuccari, Federico, 179

READ MORE IN PENGUIN

In every corner of the world, on every subject under the sun, Penguin represents quality and variety – the very best in publishing today.

For complete information about books available from Penguin – including Puffins, Penguin Classics and Arkana – and how to order them, write to us at the appropriate address below. Please note that for copyright reasons the selection of books varies from country to country.

In the United Kingdom: Please write to *Dept. EP, Penguin Books Ltd, Bath Road, Harmondsworth, West Drayton, Middlesex UB7 ODA*

In the United States: Please write to *Consumer Sales, Penguin USA, P.O. Box 999, Dept. 17109, Bergenfield, New Jersey 07621-0120.* VISA and MasterCard holders call 1-800-253-6476 to order Penguin titles

In Canada: Please write to *Penguin Books Canada Ltd, 10 Alcorn Avenue, Suite 300, Toronto, Ontario M4V 3B2*

In Australia: Please write to *Penguin Books Australia Ltd, P.O. Box 257, Ringwood, Victoria 3134*

In New Zealand: Please write to *Penguin Books (NZ) Ltd, Private Bag 102902, North Shore Mail Centre, Auckland 10*

In India: Please write to *Penguin Books India Pvt Ltd, 706 Eros Apartments, 56 Nehru Place, New Delhi 110 019*

In the Netherlands: Please write to *Penguin Books Netherlands bv, Postbus 3507, NL-1001 AH Amsterdam*

In Germany: Please write to *Penguin Books Deutschland GmbH, Metzlerstrasse 26, 60594 Frankfurt am Main*

In Spain: Please write to *Penguin Books S. A., Bravo Murillo 19, 1° B, 28015 Madrid*

In Italy: Please write to *Penguin Italia s.r.l., Via Felice Casati 20, I–20124 Milano*

In France: Please write to *Penguin France S. A., 17 rue Lejeune, F–31000 Toulouse*

In Japan: Please write to *Penguin Books Japan, Ishikiribashi Building, 2–5–4, Suido, Bunkyo-ku, Tokyo 112*

In South Africa: Please write to *Longman Penguin Southern Africa (Pty) Ltd, Private Bag X08, Bertsham 2013*

READ MORE IN PENGUIN

HISTORY

London: A Social History Roy Porter

'The best and bravest thing he has written. It is important because it makes the whole sweep of London's unique history comprehensible and accessible in a way that no previous writer has ever managed to accomplish. And it is angry because it begins and concludes with a slashing, unanswerable indictment of Thatcherite misrule' – *Independent on Sunday*

Somme Lyn Macdonald

'What the reader will longest remember are the words – heartbroken, blunt, angry – of the men who lived through the bloodbath . . . a worthy addition to the literature of the Great War' – *Daily Mail*

Aspects of Aristocracy David Cannadine

'A hugely enjoyable portrait of the upper classes . . . It is the perfect history book for the non-historian. Ample in scope but full of human detail, accessible and graceful in its scholarship, witty and opinionated in style' – *Financial Times*

The Penguin History of Greece A. R. Burn

Readable, erudite, enthusiastic and balanced, this one-volume history of Hellas sweeps the reader along from the days of Mycenae and the splendours of Athens to the conquests of Alexander and the final dark decades.

The Laurel and the Ivy Robert Kee

'Parnell continues to haunt the Irish historical imagination a century after his death . . . Robert Kee's patient and delicate probing enables him to reconstruct the workings of that elusive mind as persuasively, or at least as plausibly, as seems possible . . . This splendid biography, which is as readable as it is rigorous, greatly enhances our understanding of both Parnell, and of the Ireland of his time' – *The Times Literary Supplement*

READ MORE IN PENGUIN

HISTORY

Frauen Alison Owings

Nearly ten years in the making and based on interviews and original research, Alison Owings' remarkable book records the wartime experiences and thoughts of 'ordinary' German women from varying classes and backgrounds.

Byzantium: The Decline and Fall John Julius Norwich

The final volume in the magnificent history of Byzantium. 'As we pass among the spectacularly varied scenes of war, intrigue, theological debate, martial kerfuffle, sacrifice, revenge, blazing ambition and lordly pride, our guide calms our passions with an infinity of curious asides and grace-notes ... Norwich's great trilogy has dispersed none of this magic' – *Independent*

The Anglo-Saxons Edited by James Campbell

'For anyone who wishes to understand the broad sweep of English history, Anglo-Saxon society is an important and fascinating subject. And Campbell's is an important and fascinating book. It is also a finely produced and, at times, a very beautiful book' – *London Review of Books*

Conditions of Liberty Ernest Gellner

'A lucid and brilliant analysis ... he gives excellent reasons for preferring civil society to democracy as the institutional key to modernization ... For Gellner, civil society is a remarkable concept. It is both an inspiring slogan and the reality at the heart of the modern world' – *The Times*

The Habsburgs Andrew Wheatcroft

'Wheatcroft has ... a real feel for the heterogeneous geography of the Habsburg domains – I especially admired his feel for the Spanish Habsburgs. Time and again, he neatly links the monarchs with the specific monuments they constructed for themselves' – *Sunday Telegraph*

READ MORE IN PENGUIN

HISTORY

Citizens Simon Schama

The award-winning chronicle of the French Revolution. 'The most marvellous book I have read about the French Revolution in the last fifty years' – Richard Cobb in *The Times*

The Lure of the Sea Alain Corbin

Alain Corbin's wonderful book explores the dramatic change in Western attitude towards the sea and seaside pleasures that occured between 1750 and 1840. 'A compact and brilliant taxonomy of the shifting meanings of the sea and shore' – *New York Review of Books*

The Tyranny of History W. J. F. Jenner

A fifth of the world's population lives within the boundaries of China, a vast empire barely under the control of the repressive ruling Communist regime. Beneath the economic boom China is in a state of crisis that goes far deeper than the problems of its current leaders to a value system that is rooted in the autocratic traditions of China's past.

The English Bible and the Seventeenth-Century Revolution
Christopher Hill

'What caused the English civil war? What brought Charles I to the scaffold?' Answer to both questions: the Bible. To sustain this provocative thesis, Christopher Hill's new book maps English intellectual history from the Reformation to 1660, showing how scripture dominated every department of thought from sexual relations to political theory ... 'His erudition is staggering' – *Sunday Times*

Fisher's Face Jan Morris

'*Fisher's Face* is funny, touching and informed by wide reading as well as wide travelling' – *New Statesman & Society*. 'A richly beguiling picture of the Victorian Navy, its profound inner security, its glorious assumptions, its extravagant social life and its traditionally eccentric leaders' – *Independent on Sunday*

READ MORE IN PENGUIN

ARCHAEOLOGY

Breaking the Maya Code   Michael D. Coe

Over twenty years ago, no one could read the hieroglyphic texts carved on the magnificent Maya temples and palaces; today we can understand almost all of them. The inscriptions reveal a culture obsessed with warfare, dynastic rivalries and ritual blood-letting. 'An entertaining, enlightening and even humorous history of the great searchers after the meaning that lies in the Maya inscriptions' – *Observer*

Ancient Iraq   Georges Roux

Newly revised and now in its third edition, *Ancient Iraq* covers the political, cultural and socio-economic history of Mesopotamia from the days of prehistory to the Christian era and somewhat beyond.

Schliemann of Troy   David Traill

By uncovering what he claimed to be Homer's Troy and Mycenae, Heinrich Schliemann (1822–90) became one of the dominant personalities of his age. 'It is original, readable and gives a vivid portrait of this impossible man: belligerent, vulgar, egotistical, devious, grasping, generous, strangely impersonal and crackling with energy' – *Daily Telegraph*

Lucy's Child   Donald Johanson and James Shreeve

'Superb adventure ... *Lucy's Child* burns with the infectious excitement of hominid fever ... the tedium and the doubting, and the ultimate triumph of an expedition that unearths something wonderful about the origins of humanity' – *Chicago Tribune*

Archaeology and Language   Colin Renfrew
The Puzzle of Indo-European Origins

'The time-scale, the geographical spaces, the questions and methods of inquiry ... are vast ... But throughout this teeming study, Renfrew is pursuing a single, utterly fascinating puzzle: who are we Europeans, where do the languages we speak really stem from?' – *Sunday Times*

READ MORE IN PENGUIN

RELIGION

The Gnostic Gospels Elaine Pagels

In a book that is as exciting as it is scholarly, Elaine Pagels examines these ancient texts and the questions they pose and shows why Gnosticism was eventually stamped out by the increasingly organized and institutionalized Orthodox Church. 'Fascinating' – *The Times*

Islam in the World Malise Ruthven

This informed and informative book places the contemporary Islamic revival in context, providing a fascinating introduction – the first of its kind – to Islamic origins, beliefs, history, geography, politics and society.

The Orthodox Church Timothy Ware

In response to increasing interest among western Christians, and believing that a thorough understanding of Orthodoxy is necessary if the Roman Catholic and Protestant Churches are to be reunited, Timothy Ware explains Orthodox views on a vast range of matters from Free Will to the Papacy.

Judaism Isidore Epstein

The comprehensive account of Judaism as a religion and as a distinctive way of life, presented against a background of 4,000 years of Jewish history.

Who's Who of Religions Edited by John R. Hinnells

This detailed and informative dictionary brings together for the first time the biographies of leading men and women of religions both ancient and modern who have had a significant impact on religion.

The Historical Figure of Jesus E. P. Sanders

'This book provides a generally convincing picture of the real Jesus, set within the world of Palestinian Judaism, and a practical demonstration of how to distinguish between historical information and theological elaboration in the Gospels' – *The Times Literary Supplement*

READ MORE IN PENGUIN

ART AND ARCHITECTURE

Michelangelo: A Biography George Bull

'The final picture of Michelangelo the man is suitably three-dimensional and constructed entirely of evidence as strong as Tuscan marble' – *Sunday Telegraph*. 'An impressive number of the observations we are treated to, both in matters of fact and in interpretation, are taking their first bows beyond the confines of the world of the learned journal' – *The Times*

Painting, Power and Patronage Bram Kempers

The Italian Renaissance is one of the pinnacles of Western culture. Yet how could painters produce masterpieces for clients like the Medici, who saw art largely as a means of glorifying themselves? 'Something very remarkable happened to the position of the artist ... Kempers throws a series of challenging issues and much fascinating evidence into the historical melting pot' – *The Times Higher Education Supplement*

Strolling Through Venice John Freely

In this magnificent guide, John Freely brings Venice to life in a series of superb walks over mysterious bridges, through labyrinthine streets and into strange, almost inaccessible squares.

Ways of Seeing John Berger

Seeing comes before words. The child looks before it can speak. Yet there is another sense in which seeing comes before words ... These seven provocative essays – some written, some visual – offer a key to exploring the multiplicity of ways of seeing.

Style and Civilization

These eight beautifully illustrated volumes interpret the major styles in European art – from the Byzantine era and the Renaissance to Romanticism and Realism – in the broadest context of the civilization and thought of their times. 'One of the most admirable ventures in British scholarly publishing' – *The Times*